Gender and Macroeconomic Policy

Gender and Macroeconomic Policy

Raj Nallari and Breda Griffith

THE WORLD BANK
Washington, D.C.

ISBN: 978-0-8213-7434-4
eISBN: 978-0-8213-7435-1
DOI: 10.1596/978-0-8213-7434-4

Cover illustration: *Faces Blue*, Geoffrey Ernest Katantazi Mukasa, mixed media collage on paper, 14 5/8'' × 15 7/8''/World Bank art collection.
Cover design: Quantum Think

Library of Congress Cataloging-in-Publication Data
Nallari, Raj, 1955-
  Gender and macroeconomic policy/Raj Nallari, Breda Griffith.
    p. cm.
  Includes bibliographical references and index.
  ISBN 978-0-8213-7434-4 — ISBN 978-0-8213-7435-1 (electronic)
1. Women—Economic conditions. 2. Sexual division of labor. 3. Sex discrimination against women—Economic aspects. 4. Income distribution—Sex differences. 5. Economic policy. 6. Macroeconomics. I. Griffith, Breda. II. World Bank. III. Title.
  HQ1381.N35 2010
  339.5082—dc22

2010044906

Contents

Boxes

Figures

Tables

Preface

This volume, a compilation of lecture notes first published on the Poverty and Growth blog of the World Bank Institute in 2008–09, is an introduction to the subject of engendering macroeconomics. It aims to show how macroeconomic policies create differential opportunities for women and men. The discussion is deliberately nontechnical. Theoretical discussions and empirical evidence are brought together to give readers—policy analysts, representatives of donor agencies, and civil society organizations—a clear picture of the impact of gender relations on macroeconomic policy.

The volume comprises nine chapters covering four broad themes: gender as a category of analysis in macroeconomics; the implications of gender for macroeconomic aggregates, in particular consumption and economic growth; the role of gender in the labor market, globalization, and access to credit; and gender budgeting. Chapters 1 and 2 address the first theme. Chapter 1 focuses on the macroeconomic cost to growth and development that arises from rigid gender roles and associated gender asymmetries. Chapter 2 documents the progress made in gender mainstreaming by highlighting developments in data collection and monitoring that have moved beyond simply disaggregating data by male and female.

Chapters 3 and 4 cover the second theme. Chapter 3 considers the role of gender relations in the macroeconomic aggregates of consumption, savings, investment, and government expenditure and the implications for macroeconomic policy in these areas. Chapter 4 examines gender relations and economic growth.

Chapters 5 through 7 focus on the third theme. Chapter 5 examines the labor market (the literature is less rich for the other factor markets but is referenced throughout the volume where applicable). It also examines progress toward Millennium Development Goal (MDG) 3 and schooling issues. Chapter 6 examines how globalization affects gender relations, particularly employment. Chapter 7 concentrates on women's access to finance and documents gender asymmetries in this market.

Chapter 8, on the fourth theme, highlights the impact fiscal policies have on gender relations. It documents how policy can be made more gender specific and reports on the progress made by countries that have adopted gender-responsive government budgeting. Chapter 9 summarizes what is known about gender and macroeconomic policy, noting areas in which the literature is well developed as well as areas that require further research and study.

The lecture notes benefited from input from Laurence Clark, Pierella Paci, and G. Swamy. The financial contribution from the government of the Republic of Korea in the preparation of these notes is greatly appreciated.

About the Authors

Raj Nallari manages the Growth and Competitiveness Practice at the World Bank Institute. He holds a Ph.D. in economics from the University of Texas at Austin and has been with the World Bank since 1992. The coauthor of several books on macroeconomic stabilization, growth and poverty, and gender issues, Mr. Nallari has also written monographs for the World Bank and published articles in economic journals. He can be reached at rnallari@worldbank.org.

Breda Griffith has worked as a consultant with the World Bank Institute since 2005, mainly in the areas of growth, poverty, and gender. She holds a Ph.D. in economics from Trinity College Dublin and an M.A. in economics from the National University of Ireland. She can be reached at breda_griffith@yahoo.com.

Abbreviations

$	All dollar amounts are U.S. dollars
CIS	Commonwealth of Independent States
DHS	Demographic and Health Surveys
GAD	gender and development
GDI	Gender-related Development Index
GDP	gross domestic product
GEM	Gender Empowerment Measure
GID	Gender, Institutions and Development
GNP	gross national product
GRGB	gender-responsive government budgeting
HDI	Human Development Index
HDR	Human Development Report
ICLS	International Conference of Labor Statisticians
ILO	International Labour Organization
LFPR	labor force participation rate
MDG	Millennium Development Goal
MSE	micro- and small enterprise
NGO	nongovernmental organization
NHE	new household economics

RMSM   Revised Minimum Standard Model
ROSCA   rotating savings and credit association
SNA   System of National Accounts
WEEC   Women Economic Empowerment Consort
WID   women in development

Introduction

Mainstream economic analysis has traditionally overlooked gender. The individual—the basic category of analysis—was regarded as genderless. Neither gender discrimination nor segmentation and segregation within the labor market or the household were present.

Contributions from development theory, new household economics (NHE), labor economics, and feminist analysis have done much to change this. Focusing on gender equality—by which we mean equality in opportunity, inputs, and outcome—has yielded important insights for the growth and development of an economy. But we are still at the cusp. Although there have been huge improvements in recognizing gender as an analytical category at the microeconomic level, the macroeconomic implications of gender equality remain undeveloped.

"Engendering" macroeconomics is an important and valid research and policy area. Over the past three decades, economic development has generally affected women and men differently in the developing world. At the same time, gender relations have affected macroeconomic outcomes. This volume examines the research and policy implications of engendering macroeconomic policy. Engendering macroeconomic policy requires a deep understanding of gender equality and what it means for economic analysis at the macro level.

Chapter 1 begins with an overview of how gender—specifically, gender equality of opportunity—came to occupy an analytical category in economics. Following this overview is evidence of the significant economic and social costs to economic growth and development that arise from rigid gender roles and associated gender asymmetries. Most of the studies are from a microeconomic perspective, but the chapter draws out the implications for macroeconomics. Gender inequalities in education, health, and political representation are addressed, as are the adverse welfare effects of structural adjustment policies, which are borne primarily by women in the developing world.

Chapter 2 discusses the importance of generating appropriate data, tools, statistics, and models to assess the impact of gender relations on macroeconomic policy and vice versa. In particular, key issues of gender mainstreaming are addressed. Gender mainstreaming refers to the process of assessing the implications for women and men of all planned actions, including legislation, policies, and programs, in all areas and at all levels. Databases measuring gender equity—a recent innovation—are described and explained, and a section on the macroeconomic modeling of gender relations identifies the key ways in which models are useful for organizing knowledge and giving direction to research. The chapter concludes by noting that the approach to measuring gender has moved beyond simply disaggregating socioeconomic data on men and women to the development of databases that examine key gender issues such as participation in decision making, gender attitudes, elections, entrepreneurship, domestic violence, poverty, informal employment, time use, and school attendance.

Chapter 3 considers how behavioral outcomes based on gender have implications for key macroeconomic aggregates such as consumption, savings, investment, and government expenditure. Analysis is constrained by the lack of studies, most of which have been in the area of consumption and in the microeconomic context of the household. Nonetheless, macroeconomic conclusions can be drawn from this evidence. Research points to strong differences in gender relations and macroeconomic outcomes in developing economies. In particular, the discussion indicates that policies that improve women's control of household spending in developing economies should strengthen growth and reduce poverty.

Chapter 4 examines gender relations and economic growth. Studies cited in the chapter attest to the strong correlation between measures of gender equality and economic growth. Equality of opportunity in education, health, economics, marriage, and representation in parliament are all positively linked to economic growth. Moving beyond simple correlations, the chapter examines models of economic growth that incorporate these positive indicators for gender equality, noting that it is difficult to fully isolate the effect of gender equality on economic growth. The theoretical literature on growth and equality is reviewed from a range of perspectives, including the modernization/neoclassical approach, endogenous growth theory, the women in development approach (WID), and the gender and development approach (GAD, also known as critical feminism). The chapter concludes with a brief overview of the studies that examine the effects of economic growth and gender inequality, bringing together the conclusions of theoretical approaches from growth and feminist literature.

Chapter 5 examines gender inequality in the labor market. It looks at reasons for this inequality, including specialization, segmentation, women's reproductive roles, and wage gaps. Indicators of labor market performance by sex—labor force participation rates, unemployment rates, wage rates, and skills—are examined, as are data relating to employment by sector and status of employment. The evidence suggests a mixed story and needs to be interpreted with reference to other indicators of labor market performance, such as the increases of young women in education and older women in the labor force. The chapter finds that regional patterns are even less conclusive. It also examines the progress being made toward Millennium Development Goal 3 by considering school enrollment for boys and girls.

Chapter 6 examines some of the broad themes of globalization and its implications for women, particularly in the labor market. Trade liberalization introduces new, mostly positive prospects for women and the work they do, but gender asymmetries continue, especially with regard to wages. The impact of the recent financial crisis on employment prospects for women is also discussed.

Chapter 7 examines women's access to finance and the gender asymmetries that characterize the financial market at the level of small businesses. The literature in this area is sparse, but a number of studies at the level of the household have looked at the issue of women's access to finance and what it means for employment prospects and decision making within the household. The results from these studies may be extrapolated to inform macroeconomic policy. Microcredit, an area in which women have been targeted, is discussed.

Chapter 8 addresses gender budgeting. Making government budgeting more responsive to gender equality goals is a critical facet of gender mainstreaming. In this chapter gender budgeting initiatives are examined from the expenditure side and, to a lesser extent, the revenue side. The chapter ends with an analysis of countries' experiences with gender budgeting initiatives.

Chapter 9 brings together the four themes of engendering macroeconomics and macro policy developed in the text. Gaps in the literature and data prevent us from giving a full picture of the relationship between gender and macroeconomics—but they point the way forward for further research.

CHAPTER 1

Gender in an Economic Context

Gender refers to the social meanings that cultural mores and norms impart to biological differences between the sexes. At the same time, gender extends beyond the realms of ideology and culture into that of economics. For example, gender has historically determined the division of labor within most societies. Women have traditionally borne most of the responsibility for reproductive activities (non-income-generating activities such as the bearing and rearing of children) while also contributing to productive activities (income-generating activities normally linked to the market). Similarly, military service has traditionally been the domain of men (Çağatay 1998).

Until recently, mainstream economic analysis did not account for gender: the individual as the basic category of analysis was genderless and expected to follow a utility-maximizing course in a rational manner. Over the past few decades, gender has become an accepted category of analysis that yields important insights into economic growth and development.

Contributions from development theory and feminist analysis have done much to transform economic analysis and "engender" macroeconomic theory and policy. But despite progress in valuing and including reproductive activities in national income statistics (this has been done since the late 1970s) and in assimilating the lessons on gender inequalities from development economics, the project remains very much in its infancy.

Gender as a Category of Analysis

Benería (1995) presents an overview of gender and economics that lays the foundation for considering gender as a category of analysis. She notes that although economic analysts have explored women's issues since at least the 1930s—she cites as an early example, the "equal pay controversy" in Great Britain, which sought to understand male/female wage differentials—they did so without due consideration of gender relations.[1] Economists looked to the dynamics of the market rather than to gender relations within the market to explain wage differentials. Benería (2003, 33) notes that "the notion of the social construction of gender and its links with economic analysis had yet to be born."

The recognition of the household as an economic unit was a first step toward bringing gender into economic analysis. In the 1950s, Mincer (1980) examined women's increasing labor force participation at a time of rising family income, using the household as a category of analysis. Studies by Becker (1964, 1965, 1971), most notably, and others in the 1960s paved the way for new household economics (NHE), which acknowledged the gender division of labor and the resulting differences in labor market outcomes for household members. As Benería (1995, 1840) notes, "asymmetries in the division of labor and inequalities in the distribution of domestic work were explained through individual choices made under the assumptions of utility maximization and a harmonious household." Although the emerging literature questioned these assumptions, phrases such as "harmonious household with no conflicting interests and power relations" (Benería 1995, 1840, citing Bruce and Dwyer 1988) and the "aggregation of individual tastes and preferences within the household" (Benería 1995, 1840, citing Folbre 1988) persisted, reflecting the lack of an alternative analytical framework. Most studies continued within the neoclassical framework, using the "add women and stir" approach described by Harding (1987, cited in Benería 1995, 1840), which assumed that including women captured the dynamic and social relations between men and women. Studies that applied the theory of comparative advantage and human capital models to the analysis of specialization in home or market work were criticized for "taking as given the initial allocation of resources among household members such as the gendered skills whose acquisition and distribution feminists were questioning" (Benería 2003, 35).

The women's movement of the 1970s posed important questions about gender asymmetries. The analytical framework continued to ignore questions of gender inequality, however, concentrating instead on gender issues and how they played out in the labor market and with respect to choices in schooling.[2] During the 1980s, feminist economists began to address the inability of economic models to account for gender inequalities and gender relations (Benería 1995). These economists took a micro, interdisciplinary approach that nevertheless had implications for macroeconomics, growth, and development.[3] Some employed a Marxian approach over institutional economics. Sen's (1990) bargaining model, which allowed for cooperative conflicts within the household using game theory, was an especially important step past the rational choice models.

According to Benería (1995, 1842), the disparate approaches followed by feminist economists in the 1970s converged during the 1980s and 1990s, for a number of reasons. In particular, the political establishment's move toward the right in the United States threatened to erode the gains made by the women's movement and therefore "provided a common cause for political struggle and intellectual work." The feminist literature began considering the effects of women's social and cultural backgrounds. Because of the enormous expansion of feminist theory in the 1980s, gender emerged as a powerful category of analysis in postmodernism. By skewering traditional modes of analysis and methods of research, postmodernism transformed the humanities and the social sciences, including economics, in which its influence helped form "new questions about the discourse of economics and its androcentric biases" (Benería 1995, 1842).

In summary, mainstream economic analysis was gender blind for centuries. Because of its assumption that the household was a harmonious entity and the sum of gender-based specialization, analysis did not allow for gender discrimination, segmentation, or segregation within the labor market or inequalities within the household (Çağatay 1998). The introduction of feminist theory into labor economics and NHE paved the way for the consideration of gender as a category of analysis. As Çağatay (1998, 5–6) notes, "in these new conceptions, the point of departure for analysis was the 'real' economy as it existed, rather than the abstract thought experiments of mainstream economic theorizing about optimal behavior for the 'representative' agent with its imputed market-oriented rationality."

Gender Inequalities

Despite the progress made in recognizing gender as an analytical category at the microeconomic level, the macroeconomic implications of gender remained underdeveloped until recently. Çağatay (1998) identifies three reasons for the emergence of interest in this area:

- Economic development since the 1970s has affected women and men differently in the developing world.
- The direction of causation between macroeconomics and gender can go either way: gender relations affect macroeconomic outcomes and macroeconomic outcomes affect gender relations.
- Feminists in the 1980s pointed out that macroeconomic policies being implemented in the developing world in the context of structural adjustment policies were not gender neutral.

The academic and policy community began to recognize that a better understanding of macroeconomic outcomes for development and growth required gender-informed policies and models. Boserup's (1970) book *Women's Role in Economic Development* was one of the first studies to suggest that development policies were often gender biased. Empirical findings on the effects of gender inequalities for development and growth have given weight to that theory. Progress on including gender in macroeconomic analysis, however, has been slow.

In its 2001 study *Engendering Development*, the World Bank identified gender equality as an important development objective. Evidence in the study suggests that rigid gender roles and associated gender asymmetries have a significant negative impact on economic growth and development.

Gender inequalities primarily affect women (box 1.1). Although significant progress toward gender equality has taken place in the past 60 years, most of this progress has occurred in the developed world. Moreover, gender inequalities in basic indicators of well-being and development are greatest among the poorest households in poor countries.

Figure 1.1, reproduced from the World Bank's *Engendering Development* (2001) report, shows that gender disparities in school enrollment are greater among the poor than among the less poor. The report shows similar patterns across countries. Even after improvements in gender equality in school enrollment rates, disparities between girls and boys in school enrollment are still greater in low-income countries than in middle- and high-income countries (World Bank 2001) (figure 1.2).[4]

More recent data suggest that poverty and residence in rural areas continue to be major obstacles to girls' education. The proportion of primary school–age girls out of school in rural areas is more than twice that in urban areas (figure 1.3). Among the richest 40 percent of households,

Box 1.1

Gender Inequalities and Women

In many countries, women still lack the right to own land, manage property, conduct business, or even travel without their husbands' consent. Women continue to have systematically weaker command over a range of productive resources, including land, information, and money. Despite considerable increases in women's education relative to men, women continue to have limited opportunities and earn less than men in the labor market even when they have the same education and work experience as men. Women also remain vastly underrepresented in politics and policy making.

Source: World Bank 2001.

Figure 1.1   Male to Female Enrollment Ratio among Poorer and Richer Children 6–14 Years

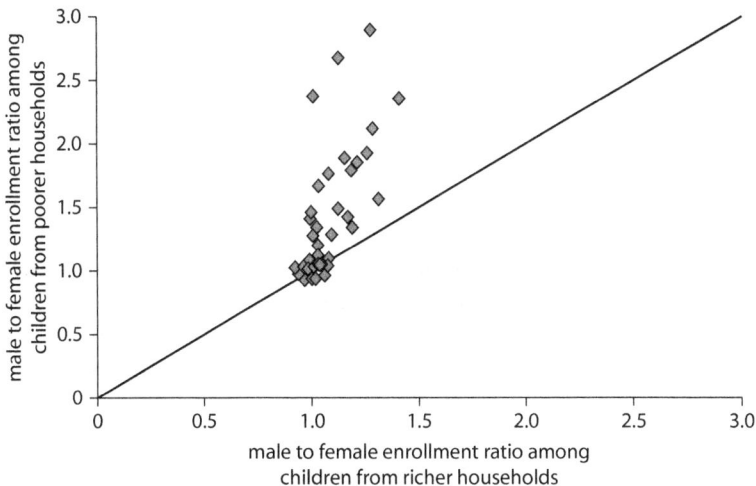

Source: World Bank 2001, citing Filmer 1999.
Note: Poorer households are defined as those in the bottom 40 percent of the wealth distribution; richer households are defined as those in the top 20 percent. The diagonal line signifies equal gender gaps within rich and poor households. Countries included are Bangladesh, Benin, Bolivia, Brazil, Burkina Faso, Cameroon, Central African Republic, Chad, Colombia, Comoros, Côte d'Ivoire, Dominican Republic, the Arab Republic of Egypt, Ghana, Guatemala, Haiti, India, Indonesia, Kazakhstan, Kenya, Madagascar, Malawi, Mali, Morocco, Mozambique, Namibia, Nepal, Nicaragua, Niger, Nigeria, Pakistan, Peru, Philippines, Rwanda, Senegal, Tanzania, Togo, Turkey, Uganda, Uzbekistan, Zambia, and Zimbabwe.

Figure 1.2   Selected Measures of Gender Equality, by Country Income Level, 1970–95

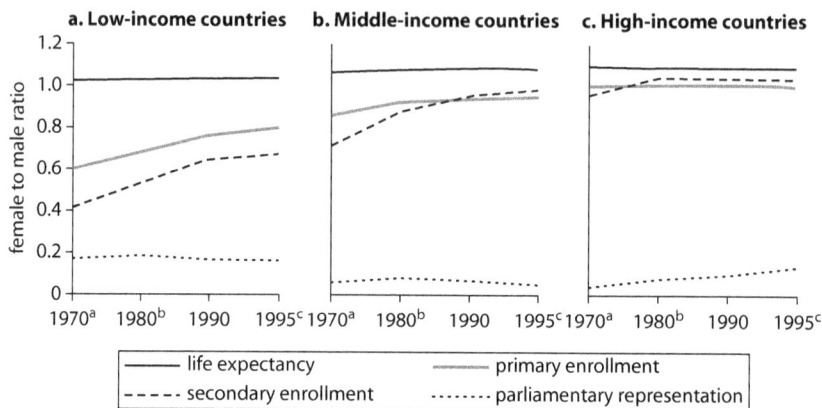

Source: World Bank 2001, 7, citing WISTAT 1998 for parliamentary data and World Bank 1999 for income data.
Note: The gross enrollment rate is enrollment in a school level, regardless of student age, expressed as a percentage of the official school-age population corresponding to that level in a given school year. The female to male enrollment ratio is the female gross enrollment ratio divided by the male gross enrollment ratio. For parliamentary representation, the ratio is seats held by women to seats held by men. All values are population-weighted averages.
a. Parliamentary data are from 1975.
b. Parliamentary data are from 1985.
c. Life expectancy data are from 1997.

1 girl in 10 is does not attend primary school; in the poorest 60 percent of households, the figure is 1 girl in 3. Although girls and boys from the richest households are almost at parity in attending primary school, there is a 5 percentage point difference between girls and boys from the poorest and richest households.

The ratio of girls to boys at all levels of education is moving closer to parity (figure 1.4). There was significant improvement in the ratio for all three levels of education between 1991 and 2008, with the greatest increases occurring in tertiary and secondary education. In 2008, 97 girls for every 100 boys were enrolled in tertiary education, up from a ratio of 67 in 1991.

Issues of gender equality and inequality have important implications for development, at both the individual and the macroeconomic level. As the World Bank (2001) notes, the foremost cost of gender inequality is its toll on the quality of human lives. Some of the findings from this report are summarized here:

• *Societies with large, persistent gender inequalities pay the price of more poverty, malnutrition, illness, and other deprivations.*

Figure 1.3   Primary School Attendance by Girls and Boys, by Income and Geographic Area, 2001–08

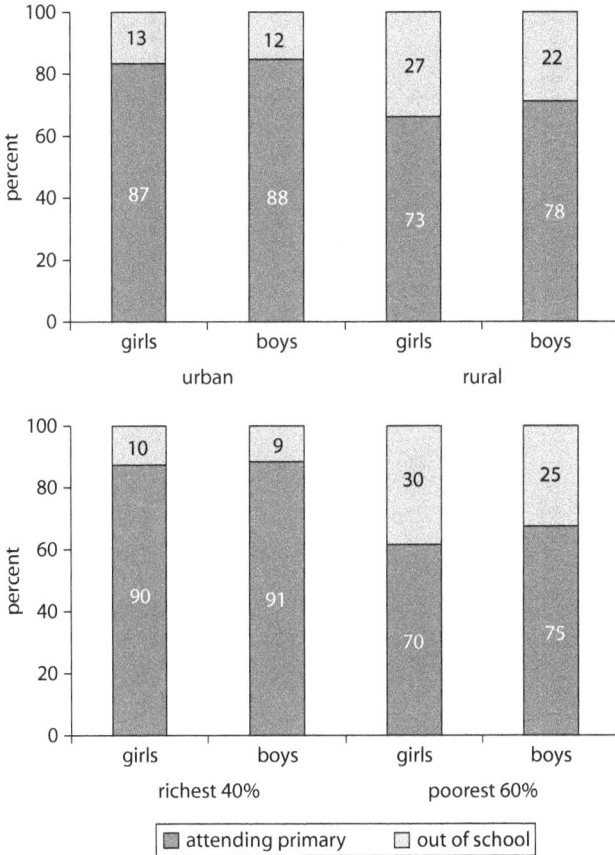

Source: United Nations 2010, 2.

- *Mothers' illiteracy and lack of schooling are detrimental to young children.* Children of illiterate or undereducated mothers experience poorer care and higher rates of malnutrition and mortality. Child immunization rates rise with a mother's education level. Under-five child mortality rates are 126 per 1,000 live births for women with no formal education, 97 for mothers with primary education, and 57 for mothers with secondary education or higher (United Nations 2010).[5]
- *Additional household income in the hands of women is likely to benefit children.* When a woman controls a household's resources, she is likely to spend more on necessities and on the development of her children than a man would in a similar situation.

Figure 1.4   Girls' versus Boys' School Enrollment in Developing Regions, 1991 and 2008

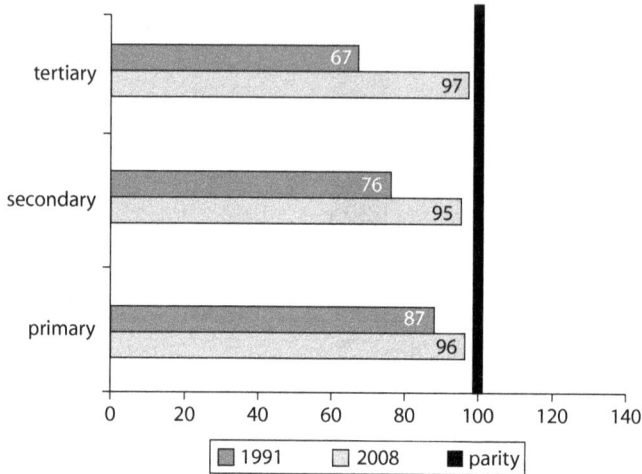

Source: United Nations 2010, 2.
Note: Figure shows number of girls per 100 boys.

- *Gender inequalities in schooling and urban jobs accelerate the spread of HIV.* HIV infection rates are higher when the gap between male and female literacy rates is wider (see also Medel-Anonuevo 2005).
- *Gender norms and stereotypes impose costs on men.* In Eastern Europe, increases in men's mortality rates were associated with increased stress and anxiety caused by high unemployment during the early years of transition.

The World Bank report also notes the detrimental effects of gender inequality on productivity, efficiency, and economic progress. By limiting the accumulation of human capital in the household and labor market and limiting women's access to resources, public services, and productive activities, gender discrimination diminishes an economy's capacity to grow and to raise living standards (World Bank 2001, 11). Research by Tzannatos (1992) shows that the elimination of gender discrimination in occupational patterns and pay could considerably increase total output. Evidence from Sub-Saharan Africa suggests that gender inequalities in the control of resources in agriculture constrain the output responses that structural adjustment policies are designed to induce (Gladwin 1991, Palmer 1991). Evidence cited by the World Bank (2001) suggests that farm yields in Burkina Faso, Cameroon, and Kenya could rise by as much as 20 percent if women and men controlled inputs and farm income more equally.

A 2010 UN study reports that just 1–3 percent of employed women in developing regions are employers and that women are less likely than men to become entrepreneurs. It attributes the low rate of entrepreneurship to cultural perceptions of the role of women and the fact that women are not permitted to own property and assets in some regions. Men are six times more likely than women to be employers in Northern Africa or Western Asia (figure 1.5).

King and Hill (1995) show that gender gaps in education adversely affect growth. As shown in figure 1.6, closing gender gaps in schooling would also accelerate economic growth. Data suggest that if in 1960 countries in the Middle East and North Africa, South Asia, and

Figure 1.5   Percentage of Employers in Total Employment, by Sex and Region, 2009

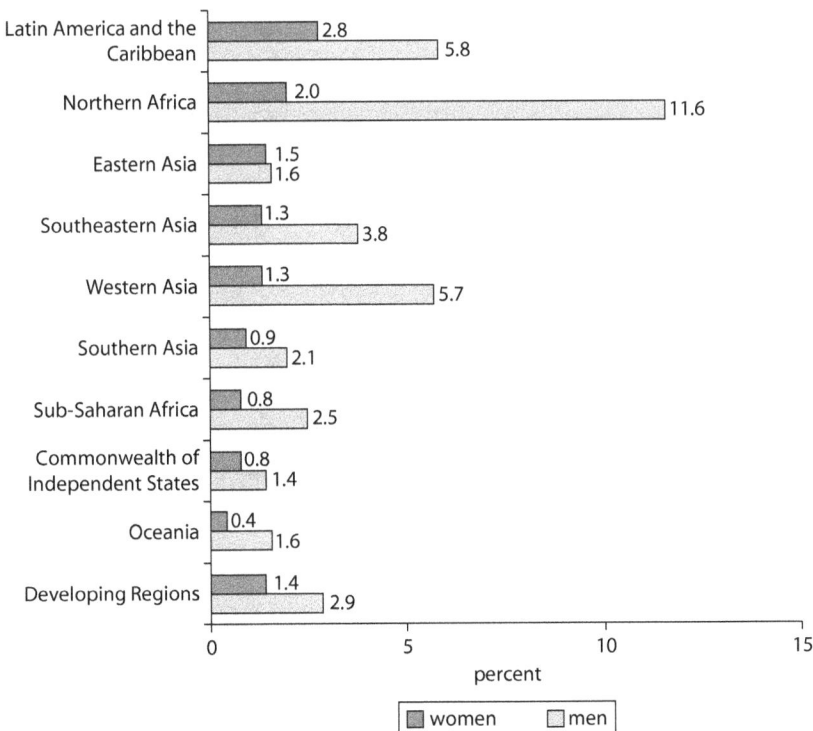

Source: United Nations 2010, 2.

Figure 1.6   Average Actual and Counterfactual Annual Growth in Per Capita GNP, by Region, 1960–92

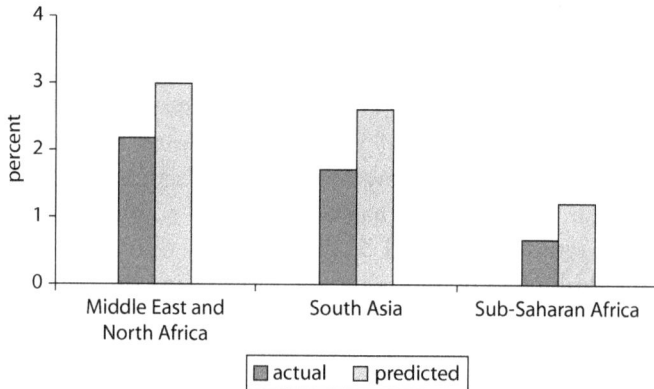

Source: World Bank 2001, 11, citing Klasen 1999.
Note: "Predicted" represents the average predicted gross national product (GNP) growth for a region if its gender gap in education had started at East Asia's level in 1960 and had narrowed as rapidly as East Asia's did from 1960 to 1992.

Sub-Saharan Africa had embarked on closing the gender gap in average years of schooling as countries in East Asia did, their per capita income would have grown by an additional 0.5–0.9 percent per year by 1992. Even for middle- and high-income countries, increasing women's share of secondary education by just 1 percent would be associated with an increase in per capita income of 0.3 percent, controlling for other growth-promoting variables.

Although developing countries as a whole have achieved near parity in tertiary enrollment, in some regions boys still outnumber girls (figure 1.7). The disparity in 2008 is especially evident in Sub-Saharan Africa (67 girls for every 100 boys) and Southern Asia (76 girls for every 100 boys). Progress in Sub-Saharan Africa has been especially poor, having increased from just 50 girls per 100 boys in 1991 to just 67 girls per 100 boys in 2008.

Public policy that promotes gender equality can help promote successful growth and development, in part by shaping individuals' decision making. These goals are in line with Millennium Development Goal (MDG) 3, to "promote gender equality and empower women," including by achieving parity with boys in secondary education. Gender equality also lies behind MDG 2 (achieving full enrollment of all children in primary education) and MDG 5 (improving maternal health).

Figure 1.7   Number of Girls per 100 Boys Enrolled in Tertiary Institutions, 1991 and 2008

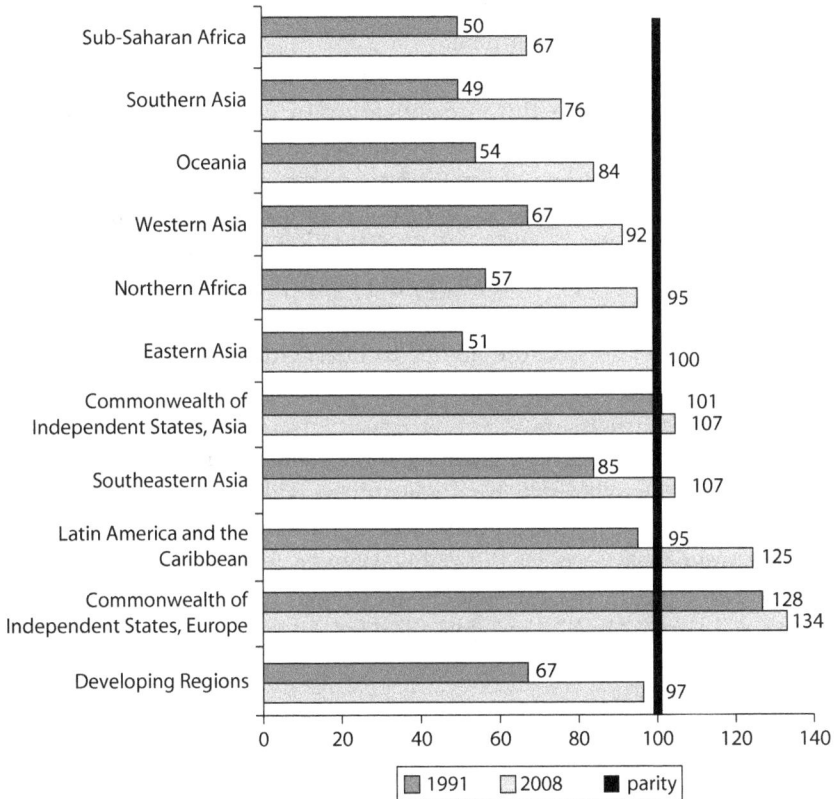

Source: United Nations 2010, 2.

Failure to consider gender issues when forming macroeconomic policies can have unintended consequences. Such was the case with the structural adjustment and macroeconomic stabilization policies of the 1980s, which suggested that countries caught in a debt spiral with severe balance of payment problems should reduce price subsidies and infrastructure investment; cut back spending on education, health, and public services; liberalize trade and capital accounts; and privatize public enterprises. The resulting shifts in resource allocation and increased productivity disproportionately affected women (Çağatay 1998) for several reasons.[6] First, structural adjustment policies led women—especially women at the lower end of the economic spectrum—to increase their participation in the labor force, but the jobs these women secured were often informal and insecure, with poor working conditions. Second, facing falling incomes, women tended to do more unpaid work in the home. The wake of these policies saw the emergence of a significant body of literature on gender and structural adjustment.

Empirical studies suggest that the "gender dimensions of the costs of adjustment range from the intensification of women's domestic and market work to the interruption of children's education (girls' in particular) to [the] increase in time inputs either to obtain basic services or self-provision. These are in addition to other costs—much less tangible and more difficult to measure—such as stress and domestic violence" (Benería 1995, 1845). Elson (1991c) argues that structural adjustment and macroeconomic stabilization policies assumed that those affected possessed the ability to deal with whatever came their way. But empirical studies have shown that women make the lion's share of the sacrifices.

Feminist economists have challenged the gender-neutral assumption in the models underlying structural adjustment and macroeconomic stabilization policies. Empirical studies show that many services—health care, for example—that were in the public domain before structural adjustment came back to the household—to women in particular—especially in poor households. The models also fail to account for the rise in women's unpaid reproductive labor, leading to socially inefficient outcomes (Elson 1995).

Çağatay, Elson, and Grown (1995, 1829) argue that ignoring gender in macroeconomic models "makes it more difficult to recognize that the welfare of the next generation may be jeopardized and the development of human resources held back." Although some progress has been made in adjusting national income statistics for gender, much crucial information remains unaccounted for, making it difficult to assess the welfare implications of macroeconomic models that use traditional indicators such as gross domestic product.[7]

Conclusion

This chapter first examined when gender became a category of analysis in economics. The emergence of NHE in the 1950s and the market implications of who controlled the household resources represented a vehicle with which to explore gender relations. A number of studies examined related topics, but for the most part the neoclassical view prevailed—the "add women and stir" approach.

Not until the 1970s were gender relations and how they might affect market outcomes and the macroeconomy really considered. During that decade, feminist literature and the women's movement questioned gender asymmetries. Data suggested that gender disparities were greater among the poor than the less poor and generally affected women more than men. Gender disparities have macroeconomic implications for children's well-being in terms of education, health, and nutrition. Failure to address gender inequalities may retard development and economic growth, leading to adverse welfare effects for future generations.

The various theoretical approaches from economics and feminist theory that recognized gender relations and gender inequalities converged in the 1980s and 1990s. The importance of engendering macroeconomics was underscored, not least because of the unintended gender biases of (structural adjustment) policies.

In summary, this chapter showed that gender relations—the socially constituted relations between women and men—have definite macroeconomic implications for growth and development.

Notes

1. Çağatay, Elson, and Grown (1995, 1828) note that "discussions of gender are often conflated with discussions of women. Gender should not, however, be read as 'pertaining to women' but should be understood as socially constituted relations between women and men."

2. Benería (1995, 1841) refers to the application of Becker's work on "racial discrimination to gender discrimination and the use of human capital theory to understand gendered choices in schooling and on research on earnings and wage differentials."

3. According to Benería (1995, 1844) the studies focused on "the nature of women's work, the labor market and the gendered divisions of labor, studies of the informal sector, employment issues in international development, the feminization of the labor force, gender and technology, the environmental crisis, migration and other demographic issues and female/male ratios and the problem of 'missing women,' among others." We discuss the macro implications of micro, interdisciplinary studies in greater detail in chapter 3.

4. During the second half of the 20th century, the primary school enrollment rates of girls roughly doubled in South Asia, Sub-Saharan Africa, and the Middle East and North Africa, rising faster than boys' enrollment rates, substantially reducing large gender gaps in schooling (World Bank 2001, 3).

5. Figures are based on surveys carried out by the United Nations in 37 developing countries during 2004–09.

6. Çağatay references Commonwealth Secretariat (1989); Standing (1989); Elson (1991b, 1991c); Moser (1992, 1996, 1998); Benería and Roldan (1987); Sen (1991); Afshar and Dennis (1992); Benería and Feldman (1992); Bakker (1994); Sparr (1994); Çağatay and Ozler (1995); Floro (1995); and Gonzales de la Rocha (1995).

7. Domestic work and voluntary activities that also represent reproductive activities in the labor market are not counted.

Bibliography

Afshar, H., and C. Dennis, eds. 1992. *Women and Adjustment Policies in the Third World*. London: Macmillan.

Bakker, I., ed. 1994. *The Strategic Silence: Gender and Economic Policy*. London: Zed Books with the North South Institute.

Becker, Gary S. 1964. *Human Capital*. New York: Columbia University Press.

———. 1965. "A Theory of the Allocation of Time." *Economic Journal* 75 (299): 493–517.

———. 1971. *The Economics of Discrimination*, rev. ed. Chicago: University of Chicago.

Beller, A. 1979. "The Impact of Equal Employment Opportunity Laws on the Male/Female Earnings Differential." In *Women in the Labor Market*, ed. C. Lloyd, E. S. Andrews, and C. L. Gilroy. New York: Colombia University Press.

Benería, L. 1995. "Toward a Greater Integration of Gender in Economics." *World Development* 23 (11): 1839–50.

———. 2003. *Gender, Development and Globalization: Economics as If All People Mattered*. New York: Routledge.

Benería, L., and S. Feldman, eds. 1992. *Unequal Burden: Economic Crises, Persistent Poverty and Women's Work*. Boulder, CO: Westview Press.

Benería, L., and M. Roldan. 1987. *The Crossroads of Class and Gender: Industrial Homework, Subcontracting and Household Dynamics in Mexico City*. Chicago: University of Chicago Press.

Benham, L. 1974. "Benefits of Women's Education within Marriage." *Journal of Political Economy* 82 (2/2): S57–S71.

Blau, F. 1976. "Longitudinal Patterns of Female Labor Force Participation." *Dual Careers* 4. U.S. Department of Labor, Washington, DC.

Boserup, E. 1970. *Women's Role in Economic Development*. London: George Allen and Unwin.

Bruce, J., and D. Dwyer, eds. 1988. *A Home Divided: Women and Income in the Third World*. Stanford, CA: Stanford University Press.

Çağatay, N. 1998. "Engendering Macroeconomics and Macroeconomic Policies." UNDP Working Paper No. 6, United Nations Development Programme, New York.

Çağatay, N., D. Elson, and C. Grown. 1995. "Introduction." *World Development* 23 (11): 1827–36.

Çağatay, N., and S. Ozler. 1995. "Feminization of the Labor Force: The Effects of Long-Term Development and Structural Adjustment." *World Development* 23 (11): 1883–94.

Commonwealth Secretariat. 1989. *Engendering Adjustment for the 1990s.* London: Commonwealth Secretariat.

Elson, D. 1991a. "Gender and Adjustment in the 1990s: An Update on Evidence and Strategies." Paper prepared for the Commonwealth Secretariat meeting on "Economic Distress, Structural Adjustment and Women," London, June 13–14.

———. 1991b. "Male Bias in the Development Process: An Overview. In *Male Bias in the Development Process*, ed. D. Elson. Manchester: Manchester University Press.

———. 1991c. "Male Bias in Macroeconomics: The Case of Structural Adjustment." In *Male Bias in the Development Process*, ed. D. Elson. Manchester: Manchester University Press.

———. 1995. "Gender Awareness in Modeling Structural Adjustment." *World Development* 23 (11): 1851–68.

Filmer, D. 1999. "The Structure of Social Disparities in Education: Gender and Wealth." Background paper for *Engendering Development*, World Bank, Washington, DC.

Floro, M. 1995. "Economic Restructuring, Gender and the Allocation of Time." *World Development* 23 (11): 1913–29.

Folbre, N. 1988. "The Black Four of Hearts: Toward a New Paradigm of Household Economics." In *A Home Divided: Women and Income in the Third World*, ed. J. Bruce and D. Dwyer. Stanford, CA: Stanford University Press.

Gladwin, C. H., ed. 1991. *Structural Adjustment and African Women Farmers.* Gainesville, FL: University of Florida Press.

Gonzales de la Rocha, M. 1995. "The Urban Family and Poverty in Latin America." *Latin American Perspectives* 22 (2): 12–31.

Harding, S., ed. 1987. *Feminism and Methodology.* Bloomington, IN: Indiana University Press.

King, E., and A. Hill. 1995. "Women's Education and Economic Well-Being." *Feminist Economics* 1 (2): 21–46.

Lloyd, C., and B. Niemi. 1979. *The Economics of Sex Differentials.* New York: Columbia University Press.

Medel-Anonuevo, C. 2005. "Addressing Gender Relations in HIV Prevention through Literacy." Paper commissioned for the *EFA Global Monitoring Report 2006, Literacy for Life.* Paris: UNESCO.

Mincer, J. 1980. "Labor Force Participation of Married Women." In *The Economics of Women and Work,* ed. A. Amsden. New York: St. Martin's Press.

Moser, C. 1992. "Adjustment from Below: Low-Income Women, Time and the Triple Role in Guayaquil, Ecuador." In *Women and Adjustment Policies in the Third World,* ed. Haleh Afshar and C. Dennis. London: Macmillan.

———. 1996. *Confronting Crises: A Comparative Study of Household Responses to Poverty and Vulnerability in Four Poor Urban Communities.* Environmentally Sustainable and Development Series and Monograph Series No. 8, World Bank, Washington, DC.

———. 1998. "The Asset Vulnerability Framework Reassessing Urban Poverty Reduction Strategies." *World Development* 26 (1): 1–19.

Palmer, I. 1991. *Gender and Population in the Adjustment of African Economies.* Geneva: International Labour Organization.

Sen, A. 1990. "Gender and Co-Operative Conflicts." In *Persistent Inequalities,* ed. I. Tinker, 195–223. New York: Oxford University Press.

Sen, G. 1991. "Macroeconomic Policies and the Informal Sector: A Gender Sensitive Approach." Working Paper 13, Vassar College, Department of Economics, Poughkeepsie, NY.

Sparr, P., ed. 1994. *Mortgaging Women's Lives: Feminist Critiques of Structural Adjustment.* London: Zed Books for the United Nations.

Standing, G. 1989. "Global Feminization through Flexible Labour." *World Development* 17 (7): 1077–96.

Stotsky, J. 2006. "Gender and Its Relevance to Macroeconomic Policy: A Survey." IMF Working Paper WP/06/233, International Monetary Fund, Fiscal Affairs Department, Washington, DC.

Tzannatos, Z. 1992. "Potential Gains from the Elimination of Labour Market Differentials." In *Women's Employment and Pay in Latin America, Part 1: Overview and Methodology,* ed. World Bank, Regional Studies Program Report 10. Washington, DC: World Bank.

United Nations. 2010. *Millennium Development Goals: Gender Equality and Women's Empowerment. Progress Chart 2010.* New York.

WISTAT (Women's Indicators and Statistics Database). 1998. *Women's Indicators and Statistics Database. Version 3.* United Nations Statistical Division, New York.

World Bank. 1999. *World Development Indicators.* Washington, DC: World Bank.

———. 2001. *Engendering Development: Through Gender Equality in Rights, Resources, and Voice.* Policy Research Report, Washington, DC.

CHAPTER 2

Measuring Gender Inequalities

The study of gender as an analytical category in macroeconomics and macroeconomic policy requires appropriate tools—data, statistics, and modeling. But gender measurement issues have been addressed only in the past 30 years or so, and much work remains to be done in this area. Data collection methods are not always gender sensitive, for a number of reasons (World Bank 2001):

- Managers, researchers, and technical staff may not be aware of or may lack experience with gender issues.
- Surveyors usually interview the household head, who is in most cases a man.
- Women may not be able or allowed to attend or speak at community meetings where gender-related issues are discussed, and formal interviews are not the best format for broaching sensitive topics (such as domestic violence).

Despite these issues, the case for measuring gender's effects is strong. In the past 20 years, national statistics-gathering programs have sought to include gender-related data, and policy makers have begun to recognize the importance of gender analysis in the development and monitoring of public policy. For the most part, however, both groups have focused almost exclusively on gathering and analyzing social and demographic statistics on gender. In fact, gender is an issue related to all statistics concerning individuals—men and women alike—and all statistical departments should be required to collect data on gender. Doing so would require the commitment of top managers in statistics-gathering bureaus and the appointment of gender advisers who would report directly to the chief statistician.

Why Measure Gender?

The World Bank (2007) has identified gender equality as a development goal in its own right, with repercussions for the long-term growth prospects of countries. Figure 2.1 illustrates how equal opportunities in rights, resources, and voice lead to economic growth.

Figure 2.1   Gender Equality, Domains of Choice, and Economic Performance: A Framework

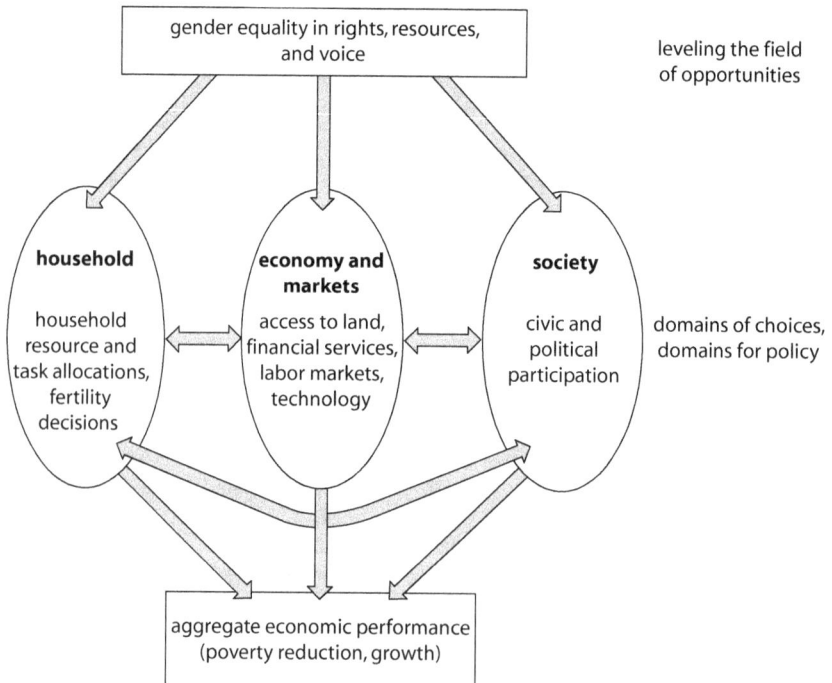

Source: World Bank 2007, 107.

Chapter 1 demonstrated the potentially negative relationship between gender inequalities and personal and economic growth and development. The literature is not conclusive on this connection however. One body of work—using the so-called modernization-neoclassical approach (Forsythe, Korzeniewicz, and Durrant 2000)—argues that economic development in general helps narrow and close the gender gap. Another (Parpart 1993; Marchand and Parpart 1995) maintains that "enduring patriarchal institutions will prevent gender equality even in the face of economic advancement" (Jütting and others 2006, 7). Saudi Arabia—a high-income country with poor gender equality—is cited as evidence of this theory.

Data on key economic, social, and political inequalities suggest that gender inequality continues. Table 2.1 shows average values of education and health indicators for three country groupings, classified by high, medium, and low levels of human development based on net enrollment as a percentage of eligible population.

Expressing gender inequality as a ratio of women to men for the relevant variables, we note that educational inequalities exist in countries with low levels of human development in primary school enrollment (0.86) and, especially, secondary school enrollment (0.73). Gender parity in both primary and secondary school enrollment is found in countries with high or medium scores on the United Nations (UN) Human Development Index (HDI), discussed below. Indeed, in the midrange countries, girls outnumber boys, at least for the year in question.

The average woman's life expectancy is higher than that of the average man, but the gap narrows in countries that score low on the HDI. Inequalities in health can be attributed to the higher mortality rate of girls and differences in life expectancy that do not accord with biological norms (Stotsky 2006). These "missing women" are a well-documented phenomenon. Comparing the sex ratios of populations with excess mortality among women to the ratios that would have prevailed without discrimination indicates that there were 90 million missing women in the early 1990s, mostly from Asian countries, in particular China and India (Klasen 1994).

Well-developed data sets are crucial to analyzing the links between levels of development and gender equality. Toward this end, a number of organizations—including the World Bank, the United Nations, and the Organisation for Economic Co-operation and Development (OECD)—have constructed databases that attempt to isolate determinants of gender inequalities. Gender statistics are important for at least

Table 2.1 Gender Ratios in Education and Health, 2001–02

(unweighted average in percent, except where otherwise indicated)

Level of human development	School enrollment, primary			School enrollment, secondary			Life expectancy at birth, 2002		
	Male ratio	Female ratio	Ratio of females to males	Male ratio	Female ratio	Ratio of females to males	Male years	Female years	Ratio of females to males
High	96	96	1.00	84	87	1.03	73.35	79.44	1.08
Medium	90	88	0.98	58	60	1.04	64.33	68.97	1.07
Low	63	55	0.86	21	15	0.73	44.69	46.52	1.04

Source: Stotsky 2006.

three reasons: (a) they bring the inequalities between women and men into the public eye, (b) they help policy makers formulate programs that address these inequalities, and (c) they provide an important baseline from which to measure and monitor the effectiveness of policy on the lives of women and men.

Traditional economic analysis, which concentrated on the market and thus income-earning activities, ignored or underestimated the unpaid, yet valuable, work of many women, including domestic and volunteer work.[1] The battle to include unpaid domestic production in the calculation of gross national product (GNP) was hard fought, even with theoretical and empirical evidence from new household economics (NHE) and the domestic labor debate. In the 1970s, however, academics, government representatives, and international organizations such as the International Labour Organization (ILO) and the United Nations spearheaded a reval- uation of women's work, redefining "economically active" to include unpaid production. At the methodological level, many countries made a commitment to improve the accuracy with which women's participation in the labor force was counted, and new techniques estimated the value of home production. The section on gender statistics below examines these approaches in further detail.

Elson (1992) argues that macroeconomic policy makers used to assume that people were able to deal with whatever economic conse- quences policies generated. In particular, the structural adjustment pro- grams of the 1980s resulted in a transfer of costs from the public sector to the private household. The underlying assumption was that women would be able to absorb these shocks by working more and "making do" on limited incomes (Elson 1993). The policies were intended to increase macroeconomic efficiency. But the failure to count a large part of the adjustment—for example, unpaid economic activities and reproductive labor, which disproportionately involve women—prevents an accurate assessment of the impact of such policies on macroeconomic efficiency, as noted in chapter 1 (Çagatay 1998).

In summary, quantifying gender is a necessary step toward making gender-related work visible and ensuring that macroeconomic policy and models foster gender equality. Quantifying gender facilitates a more accurate analysis of the unequal distribution of domestic work, productivity changes in unpaid production, shifts in domestic work and family welfare as a result of changes in family income and employment status of household members, and gross domestic prod- uct (GDP) growth (Benería 1995). The development and construction of gender-disaggregated social and economic indicators will con-tribute to more accurate macroeconomic models and therefore more informed policy.

Gender Statistics

Women's organizations and feminist scholars contend that simply dis-aggregating labor statistics and demographics by gender is insufficient and that measuring gender therefore remains a work in progress. In recent years, organizations have developed databases that quantify gender inequality in terms of opportunity—rights, resources, and voice, for example (World Bank 2001). The following paragraphs examine these databases and the progress in understanding and mea-suring women's work.

Since the 1970s, women's organizations and feminist scholars have sought to conceptualize and measure work—and women's work in particular—more accurately. Five types of work were highlighted by the United Nations Development Fund for Women (UNIFEM 2005, 25, citing Benería 1992 and UNIFEM 2000): formal market, informal market, subsistence production, unpaid care, and volunteer work. The UN System of National Accounts (SNA), which sets the international statistical standard for the measurement of the market economy, dis-tinguishes between people who are economically active and people who are economically inactive. Among those considered economically active are workers in the formal and informal markets and in the parts of subsistence production related to the production and processing of food crops.

It was not until 1993 that the SNA expanded the definition of *eco-nomically active* to include the "production of *all goods* for household consumption, including the processing and storage of all agricultural products; the production of other primary products, such as mining salt, carrying water, and collecting firewood; and other kinds of pro-cessing, such as weaving cloth and making garments, pottery, utensils, furniture, and furnishings" (UNIFEM 2005, 23). In addition, a revision to the SNA in 1993 recommended that the valuation of activities that do not fit this definition be undertaken in "satellite accounts" outside the national accounts (UNIFEM 2005, 24). The introduction of satel-lite accounts was an important step toward recognizing the economic contribution of women's unpaid care work and volunteer work, which are strongly affected by social and economic policies.[2] One way of measuring unpaid care work is through time-use surveys. These surveys gather data on how women, men, and children use their time over the course of a day. The United Nations Statistical Division (UNSD) developed an international classification of activities for time-use statistics that is sensitive to the differences between women and men, as well as boys and girls, in remunerated and unremunerated work.

The International Conference of Labor Statisticians (ICLS) agreed on an international statistical definition of the informal sector in 1993: employment and production that takes place in small or unregistered enterprises. Since then a group of organizations has expanded the definition to include self-employment in informal enterprises (small and unregistered enterprises) and wage employment in informal jobs (unregulated and unprotected jobs) for informal enterprises, formal enterprises, households, and no fixed employer.[3] The ICLS endorsed guidelines to implement this definition in 2003.

The informal sector employs more women than men in the developing world; both men and women in informal employment are more likely to be self-employed than to earn wages. Table 2.2 presents data on informal self-employment and informal wage employment.

All of the efforts described above are encompassed by the term *gender statistics*, a relatively new area of study relating to both traditional areas of statistics and the statistical system as a whole. Gender statistics facilitates an examination of gender inequalities and gender issues that goes beyond disaggregating statistics by sex. It also includes gender-specific publications and gender mainstreaming.[4] The United Nations Economic Commission for Europe (UNECE) notes the following reasons why gender statistics are needed (2004, 6–7):

- Statistics and indicators on the status of women and men are needed to formulate and monitor policies and plans, track changes, and inform the public.
- Statistical information on the situation of women and men will increase awareness about the status of women in relation to men in all spheres of society and serve as an important tool in promoting equality and monitoring progress toward achieving it.
- Gender statistics provide an impartial and comparable basis for evaluating progress toward the goals agreed upon at various World Summits to improve the situation of women.

Table 2.2   Wage and Self-Employment in Nonagricultural Informal Employment, by Sex, 1994–2000

(percentage of nonagricultural informal employment)

Region/country	Self-employment			Wage employment		
	Total	Women	Men	Total	Women	Men
North Africa	**62**	**72**	**60**	**38**	**28**	**40**
Algeria	67	81	64	33	19	36
Egypt, Arab Rep.	50	67	47	50	33	53
Morocco	81	89	78	19	11	22
Tunisia	52	51	52	43	49	48
Sub-Saharan Africa	**70**	**71**	**70**	**30**	**29**	**30**
Benin	95	98	91	5	2	9
Chad	93	99	86	7	1	14
Guinea	95	98	94	5	2	6
Kenya	42	33	56	58	67	44
South Africa	25	27	23	75	73	77
Latin America	**60**	**58**	**61**	**40**	**42**	**39**
Bolivia	81	91	71	19	9	29
Brazil	41	32	50	59	68	50
Chile	52	39	64	48	61	36
Colombia	38	36	40	62	64	60
Costa Rica	55	49	59	45	51	41
Dominican Republic	74	63	80	26	37	20
El Salvador	65	71	57	35	29	43
Guatemala	60	65	55	40	35	45
Honduras	72	77	65	28	23	35
Mexico	54	53	54	46	47	46
Venezuela, R. B.	69	66	70	31	34	30
Asia	**59**	**63**	**55**	**41**	**37**	**45**
India	52	57	51	48	43	49
Indonesia	63	70	59	37	30	41
Philippines	48	63	36	52	37	64
Syrian Arab Rep.	65	57	67	35	43	33
Thailand	66	68	64	34	32	36

Source: UNIFEM 2005, 40, citing ILO 2002.

Gender Databases

The compilation and use of gender statistics have benefited greatly from the development of databases concerned with gender inequalities and gender issues, including the following:

- participation in decision making
- gender attitudes

- participation in elections
- entrepreneurship
- domestic violence
- poverty
- informal employment
- time use
- school attendance.

Gender-related data sets identify gender inequalities in terms of inputs and outcomes. A number of gender-related databases are updated continuously as new issues are identified and new data become available. The following paragraphs examine the databases developed and maintained by the World Bank, the United Nations, and the OECD.

GenderStats

The World Bank maintains the GenderStats database, which offers statistical and other data in modules at the regional and country levels. Modules include poverty; basic demography; human development (education, health and nutrition, and population dynamics); socioeconomic roles; access to economic resources; political participation; and effects of programs and policies. Coverage is sparse for some indicators. The database draws its statistics from national statistics bureaus, UN databases, and surveys conducted or funded by the World Bank. GenderStats also includes categories for which limited or no data exist to illustrate the importance of collecting such data in the future. For example, in its educational access and attainment fields, GenderStats includes variables such as progression to grade 5 (percentage of cohort) among boys and girls, primary school completion rate (percentage of age group) among boys and girls, and youth literacy rate (percentage of people 15–24) among young men and women, with a view to populating these variables when data become available.

Gender-Related Development Index
and Gender Empowerment Measure

The United Nations Development Programme (UNDP) maintains two important databases related to gender—the Gender-related Development Index (GDI) and the Gender Empowerment Measure (GEM). The two measures, both introduced in the 1995 *Human Development Report* (*HDR*), have formed the backbone of subsequent gender-related human development analyses and policy discussions. A workshop sponsored by the *HDR* office, and marking the 10th anniversary of the indexes, sought to identify areas for improvement and to consider alternate tools for measuring gender equality. The indexes can also be applied at the national and subnational levels for ethnic and age groups.

Both measures are considered part of the HDI, which is published annually in the *HDR*.[5] The HDI measures the average achievement of a country in basic human capabilities defined as (a) a long and healthy life, as measured by life expectancy at birth; (b) knowledge, as measured by the adult literacy rate (two-thirds weight) and the combined primary, secondary, and tertiary gross enrollment ratio (one-third weight); and (c) a decent standard of living, as measured by GDP per capita in purchasing power parity (PPP) in U.S. dollars (figure 2.2).

The GDI measures achievement in the same basic capabilities as the HDI does, but it takes note of inequality in achievement between women and men. Inequality is captured by first disaggregating the three indicators of the HDI—a long and healthy life, knowledge, and a decent standard of living—by gender, resulting in male and female indexes for each indicator.[6] These indexes are adjusted by male and female population shares for each indicator, creating equally distributed indexes for all three indicators. Finally, each of the three equally distributed indexes is combined in an unweighted average to generate the GDI (see annex A for an example from Thailand).

In effect, the GDI is the HDI discounted, or adjusted downward, for gender inequality. The GDI falls when the achievement levels of both

Figure 2.2   Calculating the Human Development Index

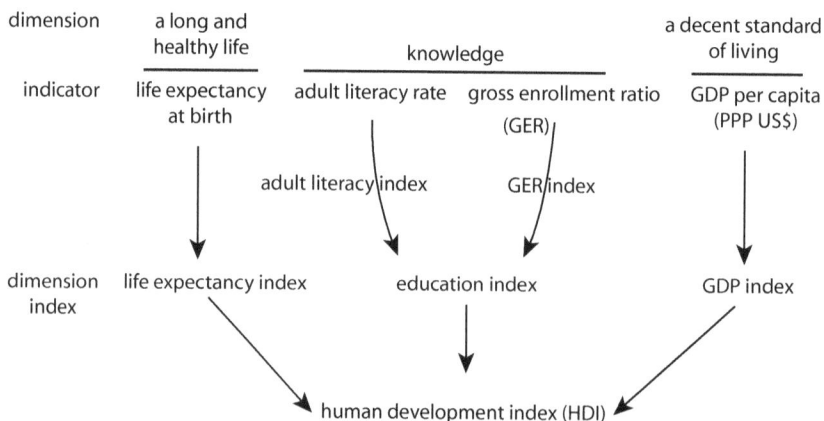

Source: UNDP 2006, Technical Note 1.

women and men in a country decrease or the disparity between their achievements increases. The greater the disparity in the basic capabilities, the lower a country's GDI compared with its HDI.

The GEM seeks to measure women's economic and political power relative to men's power in the same spheres (Klasen 2006). It is concerned with whether women can use their capabilities to take advantage of opportunities in the economic and political arenas. The GEM includes three dimensions of women's economic and political power: (a) political participation and decision-making power, as measured by the percentage of parliamentary seats held by men and women; (b) economic participation and decision making, as measured by the percentage of male and female legislators, senior officials, managers, and holders of professional and technical positions; and (c) power over economic resources, as measured by the estimated earned income of men and women. The calculation is similar to that of the HDI and GDI. An example from República Bolivariana de Venezuela is given in annex B. Data allowed for a calculation of the GEM in just 109 countries in 2009, compared with 155 countries for the GDI (UNDP 2009).

Although the GDI and GEM indexes have come under attack for various theoretical and practical reasons (discussed below), they are useful constructs and form a basis for discussing gender inequality. Table 2.3 presents the indexes for countries categorized as having high, medium, and low levels of human development based on income per capita.

As would be expected, countries with high levels of human development score high on the HDI. For countries with high and medium levels of human development, the HDI is approximately twice that of countries with low levels of human development. This is also the case for the GDI and GEM. Stotsky (2006) notes that Scandinavian countries score well on both economic and political gender equality. Developing countries score less well. In particular, countries in the

Table 2.3   Gender Inequality Indexes, 2002
(unweighted averages)

Level of human development	Human Development Index (HDI)	Gender-related Development Index (GDI)	Gender Empowerment Measure (GEM)
High	0.884	0.887	0.653
Medium	0.700	0.687	0.429
Low	0.415	0.407	0.270

Source: Stotsky 2006.

Middle East, Sub-Saharan Africa, and South Asia score low in economic and political equality.

The advantages and limitations of the GDI and the GEM have been
debated for some time and were the subject of a workshop convened by
the *HDR* office in 2006. More recently, they were a prime part of the literature review of the human development indices by Hailelul and others
(2009). This most recent review notes that the GDI reliably tracks gender
inequality in quality of life and in overall human development. The GDI
has also helped in the creation of other regional indexes and has facilitated
global comparisons (Hailelul and others 2009). But the review concurs
with previous criticisms (see Klasen 2006) that the GDI does not fully
assess gender disparity, largely because of the income indicator used in the
calculations, for which adequate data by gender do not exist. There are no
disaggregated data on male and female GDP. The income measure used in
the GDI and GEM estimates an individual's capacity to earn income. At the
same time, neither the male bias in having access to full-time paid work nor
the income earned by self-employed women is measured. Furthermore,
women in poorer countries receive lower-quality nutrition, less health care,
and fewer educational opportunities than their male counterparts. Within
the household, women are often discriminated against and have less control
over household resources than men in the same household. Discrimination
exists in the labor market, and job segmentation often positions women in
low-paying occupations. Moreover, lack of access to land and credit and the
heavy time burden associated with child-rearing and household chores,
especially among poorer women, hinder a woman's personal development
and freedom—and her economic opportunities.

The report suggests that detailed indexes, such as an individual disposable income index, be created by gender. The report also recommends
modifying the GDI to reflect specific problems faced by women in developing countries—for example, access to nutrition, housing, and clothing—and to identify sources of income (labor and rent, for example).

The review by Hailelul and others (2009) criticizes the GEM for not
capturing gender empowerment at the household level and for failing to
measure empowerment issues such as sexuality, religion, culture, and
women's rights. The GEM also fails to include some noneconomic dimensions of decision-making power, and it relies on international rather than
national databases.

UNECE Gender Statistics Database

In October 2000, the United Nations Economic Commission for Europe
(UNECE), in association with the national statistics offices of the

UNECE member countries, launched a gender statistics Web site to strengthen national capacity in the production and use of quality gender statistics, particularly in the transition economies of Eastern Europe.[7] A principal component of the Web site was the UNECE Gender Statistics Database, initiated in May 2003 to monitor gender equality and evaluate policies in all UNECE member countries. The database presents sex-disaggregated social data covering the common gender indicators—population, families and households, work and the economy, education, public life and decision making, health, and crime and violence—as well as the data series that are used to calculate these indicators (see annex C). As part of the policy component, the UNECE provides a forum for regional reviews of the Beijing Platform for Action and for the exchange of good practices in mainstreaming gender into economic policies.[8]

OECD Gender, Institutions, and Development Database

In 2006 the OECD launched its Gender, Institutions and Development (GID) database. The GID expands on the work of the other databases discussed by including information on social institutions that affect gender equality. "Construction of the GID database follows a clear conceptual framework that differentiates between outcome and input variables: the former measure the extent to which women suffer discrimination (for example, women's participation in the labor force) and the latter encompass underlying reasons for this discrimination" (Jütting and others 2006, 9). Figure 2.3 outlines the framework for the construction of the GID. The focus of the GID is on the solid circuit, which describes four channels through which social institutions influence the economic role of women.

According to the diagram, social institutions directly affect women's economic roles (the link from A to D); social institutions can also indirectly affect how fully women participate in the economy. Figure 2.3 identifies two such channels. For example, a woman's greater physical integrity improves her health and consequently her chances in the labor market (A to B to D). Social institutions can also encourage a country's economic development, which, in turn, increases women's labor force participation (A to C to D). Social institutions can also affect women's roles more indirectly, by improving their access to resources—such as health and education—which in turn improves economic development (A to B to C to D or A to C to B to D) (Jütting and others 2006, 10).

The conceptual framework described in figure 2.3 requires an outcome variable that measures women's participation in the economy. The outcome variable used is women's paid labor, based on the assumption

Figure 2.3   Input and Output Variables Affecting the Economic Role of Women

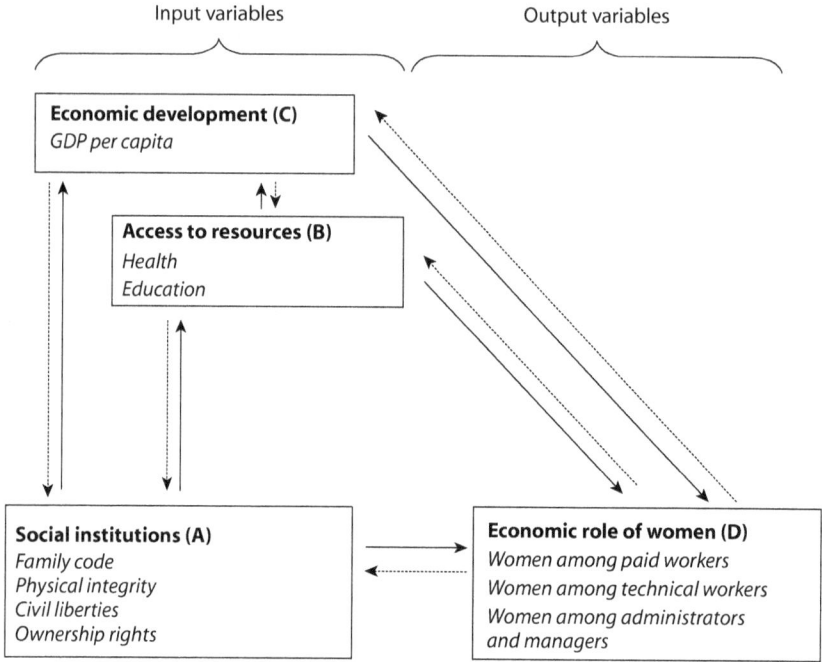

Source: Jütting and others 2006, 10.

that "women in a country are 'better-off' the higher the rate of women's participation in paid work" (Jütting and others 2006, 11).

There are 162 countries in the GID database, although data on social institutions are available for only some of these countries. The GID focuses on gender-related differences; hence most of the variables are measured in terms of ratios. Figure 2.4 shows the regional indexes of discrimination against women for the four measures of social institutions identified in figure 2.3.

The World Bank, the ILO, and the World Health Organization (WHO) provide the data on access to resources, economic development, and the economic role of women. The OECD also uses the GDI and GEM. Data on social institutions are not readily available and are therefore derived from many sources. They include both quantitative and qualitative variables from Amnesty International; BRIDGE, a research and information service of the Institute for Development Studies (IDS) that specializes in gender and development; the Women in Development Network

Figure 2.4   Indexes of Discrimination against Women, by Region

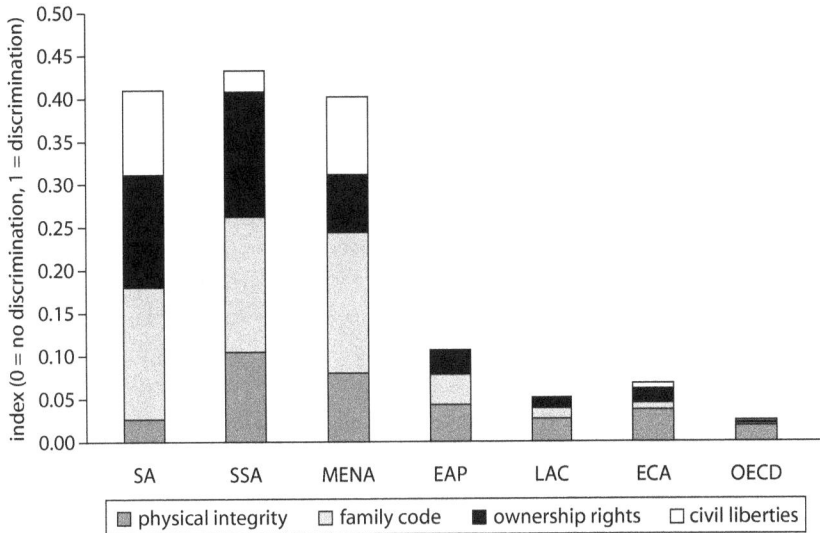

Source: Jütting and others 2006, 20.
Note: Data are for various years between 2002 and 2005. SA = South Asia; SSA = Sub-Saharan Africa;
MENA = Middle East and North Africa; EAP = East Asia and Pacific; LAC = Latin America and the Caribbean;
ECA = Europe and Central Asia. Physical integrity measures the extent of female genital mutilation and the existence of legislation punishing acts of violence against women. Family code pertains to marriage before the age
of 20, acceptance of polygamy within a society, unequal parental authority of fathers and mothers, and inheritance
practices that favor male heirs. Ownership rights pertain to women's access to land ownership, bank loans, and
property other than land. Civil liberties refer to freedom of movement and obligation to wear a veil in public.

(WIDNET); AFROL, a news agency that concentrates on Africa; and a
study commissioned by the French Parliament (Lang 1998), among others.[9] The database also draws on gender profiles from various donor agencies, such as the Canadian International Development Agency (CIDA).

Engendering Macroeconomic Models

Çağatay (1998, 11) identifies four ways in which macroeconomic models
can be "gender aware." The gender-disaggregation method involves disaggregating existing macroeconomic variables by gender. This first method
depends on the structure of the economy. For example, disaggregating
investment by gender in an economy dominated by small producers
yields more information than doing so in one dominated by large private
or public enterprises, in which "gender differences in behavior will be

more subtle and less uniform" (Çağatay 1998, 12). This method is best suited to economies in which men and women control separate streams of income and undertake separate productive investments. Because gender-disaggregation models do not include the reproductive sector, they cannot take into account the causal links between this sector and the productive sector. In terms of precedent, the gender-disaggregation approach may be modeled in the way that class is modeled in classical and post-Keynesian macroeconomic models. In the post-Keynesian models, the savings behaviors of capitalists and workers are considered different because of their different institutional positions.

The second method, the gendered macroeconomic variable, introduces economic variables that reflect gender relations. For example, gender inequality is thought to influence behavior in labor markets, credit markets, household decision making, and the public and private sectors (Çağatay, Elson, and Grown 1995, 1830). Taking this influence into account will change the outcome of the model and the resulting policy prescriptions. Referencing a standard macroeconomic model, such as the Revised Minimum Standard Model (RMSM) of the World Bank, and introducing unpaid labor changes, the value of the capital to output ratio—a ratio that is considered the principal gauge of overall efficiency. Similarly, the savings rate is known to have clear gender dimensions; allowing for these dimensions in macroeconomic models would yield different outcomes for consumption and the overall savings rate.

The third approach is the two-sector system method, which divides the economy into productive and reproductive sectors. The productive sector includes traditional macroeconomic variables; the reproductive sectors include unpaid labor, nonmonetized goods and services, and human resource networks. Such models focus on the interactions between the two sectors. Çağatay (1998) references Taylor (1995), who examines the relationships between the variables in the two sectors using a social accounting matrix.

The fourth approach involves combining two or more of the methods described above. Table 2.4 summarizes two studies that make use of two of these methods.

Conclusion

Failure to quantify gender relations can allow gender inequalities to go unchecked, with adverse implications for a country's economic growth and development. In this chapter, we first make the case that fully appreciating

Table 2.4 Examples of Use of More than One Macroeconomic Model in Studying Gender Relations

Author/year	Objective	Hypothesis	Methodology	Result
Darity (1995)	Divide economy into two sectors: the household sector, in which production is carried out by women, and the cash-crop sector, in which activities are gender specific (men control production process and income from cash crop; pulling women from household when needed).	The loss of female labor to the cash-crop sector affects output of the household sector.	Method 1 and method 3	In a gender-segregated, low-income economy in which women are expected to be flexible across sectors and shoulder the time and work burden, an export boom may cause nutritional deprivation for women.
Erturk and Çağatay (1995)	Examine how secular changes (greater participation by women) and cyclical changes in the feminization of the labor force and intensity of female household labor influence the behavior of macroeconomics.	An increase in the feminization of the labor force is likely to have a positive effect on investment; the savings rate is positively related to the intensity of female household labor.	Growth cycle model; method 2	An economic recovery in the monetary sector is likely to succeed when the impact of the feminization of the labor force on investment is stronger than the impact of the intensity of female household labor on savings.

Source: Çağatay 1998.

gender as an analytical category requires appropriate data and tools. Gender measurement issues have been addressed only in the past 30 years, and databases measuring gender equality are far more recent.

Although measuring gender remains a work in progress, significant efforts have been made in recent decades. Previously, economists simply disaggregated socioeconomic data by male and female. Doing so is just a first step toward measuring gender; it does not capture the effects of gender relations. The development of a number of databases marked another step forward. These databases incorporate key gender issues, such as participation in decision making, gender attitudes, participation in elections, entrepreneurship, domestic violence, poverty, informal employment, time use, and school attendance. This chapter shows how these databases identify gender inequalities in terms of inputs and outcomes and why this information is useful for policy makers. The chapter concludes by presenting a number of potential approaches for the macroeconomic modeling of gender relations.

In summary, this chapter describes recent and ongoing efforts to quantify gender relations, the impetus for which was explained in chapter 1. It provides a basis for examining the implications of gender relations and gender inequalities for the macroeconomic variables of consumption and saving, the subject of chapter 3.

Annex A: Calculating the Gender-Related Development Index (GDI) for Thailand

Calculating the Equally Distributed Life Expectancy Index

The first step is to calculate separate indices for women's and men's life expectancy, using the general formula for dimension indexes:

Women

Life expectancy: 73.2 years

Life expectancy index $= \dfrac{73.2 - 27.5}{87.5 - 27.5} = 0.762$

Men

Life expectancy: 64.9 years

Life expectancy index $= \dfrac{64.9 - 22.5}{82.5 - 22.5} = 0.707.$

Next, the two indexes are combined to create the equally distributed life expectancy index, using the general formula for equally distributed indexes:

Women

Population share: 0.508
Life expectancy index: 0.762

Men

Population share: 0.492
Life expectancy index: 0.707

Equally distributed life expectancy index $= \{[0.508\,(0.762^{-1})] + [0.492\,(0.707^{-1})]\}^{-1} =$ **0.734.**

Calculating the Equally Distributed Education Index

First, indices for the adult literacy rate and the combined primary, secondary, and tertiary gross enrollment ratio are calculated separately for women and men. Calculating these indexes is straightforward, as the indicators used are already normalized between 0 and 100.

Women

Adult literacy rate: 94.1%
Adult literacy index: 0.941
Gross enrollment ratio: 69.3%
Gross enrollment index: 0.693

Men

Adult literacy rate: 97.3%
Adult literacy index: 0.973
Gross enrollment ratio: 74.6%
Gross enrollment index: 0.746

Second, the education index, which assigns two-thirds weight to the adult literacy index and one-third weight to the gross enrollment index, is computed separately for females and males:

Education index = 2/3 (adult literacy index) + 1/3 (gross enrollment index)
Women's education index = 2/3 (0.941) +1/3 (0.693) = 0.858
Men's education index = 2/3 (0.973) + 1/3 (0.746) = 0.897.

Finally, the two education indexes are combined to create the equally distributed education index:

Women
Population share: 0.508
Education index: 0.858

Men
Population share: 0.492
Education index: 0.897

Equally distributed education index = $\{[0.508 \ (0.858^{-1})] + [0.492 \ (0.897^{-1})]\}^{-1}$ = **0.877.**

Calculating the Equally Distributed Income Index

First, earned income (in purchasing power parity [PPP]) is estimated for women and men. The income index is then calculated for each group. Income is adjusted by taking the logarithm of estimated earned income:

$$\text{Income index} = \frac{\log (\text{actual value}) - \log (\text{minimum value})}{\log (\text{maximum value}) - \log (\text{minimum value})}.$$

Women
Estimated earned income (PPP): $4,875
$\text{Income index} = \dfrac{\log (4,875) - \log (100)}{\log (40,000) - \log (100)} = 0.649$

Men
Estimated earned income (PPP): $7,975
$\text{Income index} = \dfrac{\log (7,975) - \log (100)}{\log (40,000) - \log (100)} = 0.731.$

Second, the income indexes for women and men are combined to create the equally distributed income index:

Women
Population share: 0.508
Income index: 0.649

Men
Population share: 0.492
Income index: 0.731

Equally distributed income index = $\{[0.508 \ (0.649^{-1})] + [0.492 \ (0.731^{-1})]\}^{-1}$ = **0.687.**

Calculating the GDI

Calculating the GDI is straightforward. It is simply the unweighted average of the three component indexes—the equally distributed life expectancy index, the equally distributed education index, and the equally distributed income index:[10]

$$\text{GDI} = 1/3 \ (\text{life expectancy index}) + 1/3 \ (\text{education index}) + 1/3 \ (\text{income index})$$
$$= 1/3 \ (0.734) + 1/3 \ (0.877) + 1/3 \ (0.687) = \textbf{0.766}.$$

Way $\varepsilon = 2$ in Calculating the GDI

The value of ε is the size of the penalty for gender inequality. The larger the value, the more heavily a society is penalized for having inequalities.

If $\varepsilon = 0$, gender inequality is not penalized (in this case the GDI would have the same value as the human development index). As ε increases toward infinity, more and more weight is given to the lower achieving group.

The value 2 is used in calculating the GDI (as well as the GEM). This value places a moderate penalty on gender inequality in achievement. For a detailed analysis of the mathematical formulation of the GDI, see Anand and Sen (1995) and Bardhan and Klasen (1999); and the technical notes in and UNDP 1995 and 1999.

Source: UNDP 2003, 343.

Annex B: Calculating the Gender Empowerment Measure (GEM) for República Bolivariana de Venezuela

Calculating the Equally Distributed Equivalent Percentage (EDEP) for Parliamentary Representation

The EDEP for parliamentary representation measures the relative empowerment of women in terms of their political participation. It is calculated using the women's and men's shares of the population and their respective shares of parliamentary seats according to the general formula.[10]

Women

Population share: 0.497
Parliamentary share: 9.7%

Men

Population share: 0.503
Parliamentary share: 90.3%

EDEP far parliamentary representation = $\{[0.497\,(9.7^{-1})] + [0.503\,(90.3^{-1})]\}^{-1} = 17.60$.

This initial EDEP is then indexed to an ideal value of 50%.

Indexed EDEP for parliamentary representation $= \dfrac{17.60}{50} = \mathbf{0.352.}$

Calculating the EDEP for Economic Participation

Using the general formula, an EDEP is calculated for women's and men's percentage shares of positions as legislators, senior officials, and managers. Another is calculated for their respective percentage shares of professional and technical positions. The simple average of the two measures gives the EDEP for economic participation.

Women

Population Share: 0.497
Share of positions as legislators, senior officials, and managers: 24.3%
Share of professional and technical positions: 57.6%

Men

Population share: 0.503
Share of positions as legislators, senior officials, and managers: 75.7%
Share of professional and technical positions: 42.4%

EDEP for positions as legislators, senior officials, and managers = $([0.497\,(24.3^{-1})] + [0.503\,(75.7^{-1})]\}^{-1} = 36.90$.

Indexed EDEP for positions as legislators, senior officials, and managers $= \dfrac{36.90}{50} = 0.738$.

EDEP for professional and technical positions = $\{[0.497\,(57.6^{-1})] + [0.503\,(42.4^{-1})]\}^{-1} = 48.80$.

Indexed EDEP for professional and technical positions $= \dfrac{48.80}{50} = 0.976$.

The two indexed EDEPs are averaged to create the EDEP for economic participation:

EDEP for economic participation $= \dfrac{0.738 + 0.976}{2} = \mathbf{0.857.}$

Calculating the EDEP for Income

Earned income (in purchasing power parity [PPP]) is estimated for women and men separately and then indexed to goalposts. The income index is based on unadjusted values, not the logarithm of estimated earned income (as used to calculate the GDI).

Women

Population share: 0.497
Estimated earned income (PPP): $3,288

$$\text{Income index} = \frac{3{,}288 - 100}{40{,}000 - 100} = 0.080$$

Men

Population share: 0.503
Estimated earned income (PPP): $8,021

$$\text{Income index} = \frac{8{,}021 - 100}{40{,}000 - 100} = 0.199.$$

The female and male indexes are then combined to create the equally distributed index:

$$\text{EDEP for income} = \{[0.497\,(0.080^{-1})] + [0.503\,(0.199^{-1})]\}^{-1} = \mathbf{0.114}.$$

Calculating the GEM

Once the EDEP has been calculated for the parlimentary representation, economic participation, and income, determining the GEM is straightforward. It is a simple average of the three EDEP indexes.

$$\text{GEM} = \frac{0.352 + 0.857 + 0.114}{3} = \mathbf{0.441}.$$

Source: UNDP 2003, 345.

Annex C: Databases of Common Gender Indicators

Table 2C.1   Databases of Common Gender Indicators

Indicator	Database
Population	Population of five-year age groups by age, male/female, country, and year
	Population of selected age groups by male/female, country, and year
	Sex ratio for population age 80 and over by country and year
	Population of five-year age groups by marital status, age, male/female, country, and year
	Population of selected age groups 18 and over by marital status, age, male/female, country, and year
Families and households	Live births by mother's age, country, and year
	Total fertility rate by country and year
	Adolescent fertility rate by country and year
	Mean age of women at birth of first child by country and year
	Mean age at first marriage by male/female, country, and year
	Legal abortions by country and year
	One-parent families and children by sex of parent, country, and year
	Private households by household type, country and year
	One-person households by age, male/female, country, and year
Work and the economy	Labor force by age, male/female, country, and year
	Employment by sector of activity, male/female, country, and year
	Employment by occupation, male/female, country, and year
	Employment in public and private sector by sector of activity, male/female, country, and year
	Employment by status of employment, male/female, country, and year
	Part-time employment by male/female, country, and year
	Unemployment by age, male/female, country, and year
	Youth unemployment by male/female, country, and year
	Long-term unemployment by male/female, country, and year
	Unemployed by age, reason, male/female, country, and year
	Gender pay gap by level of education, country, and year
Education	Upper secondary and postsecondary students by male/female, country, and year
	Enrollment ratio at secondary level by male/female, country, and year
	Educational attainment by male/female, country, and year
	Graduates by type of program, male/female, country, and year
	Tertiary students by field of study, type of program, male/female, country, and year
	Teachers by level of education, male/female, country, and year
	Percentage of population in lifelong learning by male/female, country, and year

(continued)

Table 2C.1   Databases of Common Gender Indicators *(continued)*

Indicator	*Database*
Public life and decision making	Members of national parliament by male/female, country, and year
	Government ministers by male/female, country, and year
	Senior-level civil servants by male/female, country, and year
	Members of municipal councils or other local area governing bodies by male/female, country, and year
	Judges by male/female, country, and year
	Central bank board members by male/female, country, and year
	Chief editors of national newspapers by male/female, country, and year
	Journalists by male/female, country, and year
	Heads of universities by male/female, country, and year
Health	Life expectancy by age, male/female, country, and year
	Probability of dying between age 15 and 59 by male/female, country, and year
	Infant mortality rate by male/female, country, and year
	Deaths per 1,000 among children age 1–4 by male/female, country, and year
	Smokers, as percent of population, by age, male/female, country, and year
	Population by level of body mass index by weight, age, male/female, country, and year
Crime and violence	Victims of crime by type of crime, male/female, country, and year
	Persons convicted by age, male/female, country, and year
	Convictions by conviction type, male/female, country, and year
	Men convicted for rape and attempted rape as a percent of all convicted men by country and year
	Prisoners by recidivist status, male/female, country, and year
	Foreign prisoners by male/female, country, and year

Source: UNECE Web site, http://www.unece.org.

Notes

1. Four components of work are affected by undercounting: voluntary activities and domestic work, subsistence, production, and the informal sector. Production and the informal sector have been included in the national income accounts of most countries since the 1950s. Before the 1980s, the economic case for including volunteer activities and domestic work in official statistics was weak.

2. *Care work* refers to the provision of services within households for other household and community members. *Unpaid care work* avoids the ambiguities of terms such as *domestic labor,* which can also refer to the work of paid domestic workers; *unpaid labor,* which can also refer to unpaid work in the family business; *reproductive work,* which can also refer to giving birth and

breastfeeding; and *home work*, which can also refer to paid work done in the home on subcontract from an employer (UNIFEM 2005, 24).

3. The ILO, the International Expert Group on Informal Sector Statistics (the Delhi Group), and the Women in Informal Employment: Globalizing and Organizing (WIEGO) network worked together to expand the definition of informal work.

4. Gender mainstreaming is discussed in chapter 6. As noted by the UNECE (2004, i), "gender statistics plays a crucial role in mainstreaming gender into policies by documenting the different ways in which policies, social norms, and cultural values impact the lives of women and men."

5. The HDI comprises five measures: the Human Development Index itself (HDI), the Gender-related Development Index (GDI), the Gender Empowerment Measure (GEM), the Human Poverty Index for developing countries (HPI-1), and the Human Poverty Index for OECD countries (HPI-2).

6. Women's longer life expectancy is taken into consideration in the calculations.

7. UNECE member countries include Albania, Andorra, Armenia, Austria, Azerbaijan, Belarus, Belgium, Bosnia and Herzegovina, Bulgaria, Canada, Croatia, Cyprus, the Czech Republic, Denmark, Estonia, Finland, France, Georgia, Germany, Greece, Hungary, Iceland, Ireland, Israel, Italy, Kazakhstan, the Kyrgyz Republic, Latvia, Liechtenstein, Lithuania, Luxembourg, Macedonia, Malta, Moldova, Monaco, Montenegro, the Netherlands, Norway, Poland, Portugal, Romania, the Russian Federation, San Marino, Serbia, the Slovak Republic, Slovenia, Spain, Sweden, Switzerland, Tajikistan, Turkey, Turkmenistan, Ukraine, the United Kingdom, the United States, and Uzbekistan.

8. At the Fourth World Conference on Women, UN member states adopted and committed to implement the Beijing Platform for Action, which identifies 12 critical areas of concern with respect to the advancement of women and the achievement of gender equality. Worldwide progress in the implementation of the Beijing Platform for Action is reviewed every five years by the Commission on the Status of Women (see http://www.unece.org/gender).

9. Most of the qualitative variables vary between 0 (better) to 1 (worse) (Jütting and others 2006, 11).

10. The general formula for the equally distributed index is: Equally distributed index = {[female population share (female index$1-\varepsilon$)] + [male population share (male index$1-\varepsilon$)]}$1/1-\varepsilon$ where ε measures the aversion to inequality.

Bibliography

Anand, Sudhir, and Amartya Sen. 1995. *Gender Inequality in Human Development: Theories and Measurement.* Occasional Paper 12. United Nations Development Programme, Human Development Report Office, New York.

Bardhan, Kalpana, and Stephen Klasen. 1999. "UNDP's Gender-Related Indices: A Critical Review." *World Development* 27 (6): 985–1010.

Benería, L. 1992. "Accounting for Women's Work: The Progress of 2 Decades." *World Development* 20 (11): 1547–60.

———. 1995. "Toward a Greater Integration of Gender in Economics." *World Development* 23 (11): 1839–50.

Çağatay, N. 1998. "Engendering Macroeconomics and Macroeconomic Policies." UNDP Working Paper 6, United Nations Development Programme, New York.

Çağatay, N., D. Elson, and C. Grown. 1995. "Introduction." *World Development* 23 (11): 1827–36.

Darity, W. 1995. "The Formal Structure of a Gender-Segregated Low-Income Economy." *World Development* 23 (11): 1963–68.

Elson, D. 1992. "From Survival Strategies to Transformation Strategies: Women's Needs and Structural Adjustment." In *Unequal Burden: Economic Crises, Persistent Poverty and Women's Work*, ed. L. Benería and S. Feldman. Boulder, CO: Westview Press.

———. 1993. "Gender-Aware Analysis and Development Economics." *Journal of International Development* 5 (2): 237–47.

Erturk, K., and N. Çağatay. 1995. "Macroeconomic Consequences of Cyclical and Secular Changes in Feminization: An Experiment at Gendered Modeling." *World Development* 23 (11): 1969–77.

ESCE (Economic Social Council of Europe). 2006. "Gender Sensitization Training for Statisticians." Capacity Building Program on Engendering National Statistics Systems for a Knowledge-Based Policy Formulation in CIS and SEE Countries, Note by Secretariat and the World Bank Institute, Geneva.

Forsythe, N., R. P. Korzeniewicz, and V. Durrant. 2000. "Gender Inequalities and Economic Growth: A Longitudinal Evaluation." *Economic Development and Cultural Change* 48 (3): 573–617.

Hailelul, S., A.A. Iyasu, V. Tcherniak, and M. Urek, 2009. *Critical Literature Review of the Human Development Indices.* Report prepared for the UNDP Practicum in International Affairs. New York. http://www.gpia.info/files/practicum/28/UNDP%20HDR.ppt.

ILO (International Labour Organization). 2002. *Women and Men in the Informal Economy: A Statistical Picture.* Geneva: ILO.

Jütting, J. P., C. Morrisson, J. Dayton-Johnson, and D. Drechsler. 2006. "Measuring Gender (In)Equality: Introducing the Gender, Institutions and Development Database (GID)." Working Paper No. 247, OECD Development Centre, Organisation for Economic Co-operation and Development. Paris.

Klasen, S. 1994. "Missing Women Reconsidered." *World Development* 22 (7): 1061–71.

————. 2006. *Measuring Gender Inequality and Its Impact on Human Development: The Debate about the GDI and GEM.* United Nations Development Programme, Human Development Report Office, New York.

Lang, J. 1998. *Enquête sur la situation des femmes dans le monde.* Assemblée Nationale, Paris.

Marchand, M. H., and J. L. Parpart, eds. 1995. *Feminism, Postmodernism Development.* London: Routledge.

Parpart, J. L. 1993. "Who Is the Other? A Postmodern Feminist Critique of Women and Development Theory and Practice." *Development and Change* 24 (3): 439–64.

Stotsky, J. 2006. "Gender Budgeting." IMF Working Paper WP/06/232, Fiscal Affairs Department, International Monetary Fund, Washington, DC.

Taylor, L. 1995. "Environmental and Gender Feedbacks in Macroeconomics." *World Development* 23 (11): 1953–61.

UNDP (United Nations Development Programme). 1995. *Human Development Report 1995: Gender and Development.* New York: Oxford University Press.

————. 1999. *Human Development Report 1999: Globalization with a Human Face.* New York: Oxford University Press.

————. 2003. *Human Development Report: Millennium Development Goals: A Compact among Nations to End Human Poverty.* New York: Oxford University Press.

————. 2005. *Human Development Report 2005: International Cooperation at a Crossroads: Aid, Trade and Security in an Unequal World.* Gender-Related Development Index (GDI) and Gender Empowerment Measure (GEM). New York: Oxford University Press.

————. 2006. *Global Human Development Report. Beyond Scarcity: Power, Poverty and Global Water Crisis.* New York: UNDP.

————. 2009. *Human Development Report. Overcoming Barriers: Human Mobility and Development.* New York: UNDP.

UNECE (United Nations Economic Commission for Europe). 2004. *Report on the Status of Official Statistics Related to Gender Equality in Eastern Europe and the CIS Countries.* UNECE Statistical Division and UNDP Bratislava Regional Center, Geneva.

UNIFEM (United Nations Development Fund for Women). 2000. *Progress of the World's Women.* New York: UNIFEM.

————. 2005. *Progress of the World's Women 2005: Women, Work and Poverty.* New York: UNIFEM.

World Bank. 2001. *Engendering Development through Gender Equality in Rights, Resources and Voice.* Washington, DC: World Bank.

————. 2007. *Global Monitoring Report 2007.* Washington, DC: World Bank.

CHAPTER 3

Gender and Macroeconomic Aggregates

Differences in the behavior of men and women may lead to different macroeconomic outcomes, particularly for aggregates such as private consumption, savings and investment, and the composition of government expenditure. As a result, gender budgeting has become an important issue in most countries over the past few decades. Chapter 8 examines the gender budgeting methods and outcomes in a number of countries. This chapter explores gender's influence on consumption and saving. We first contextualize the discussion by examining the linkages between the household and its gender composition and macroeconomic aggregates.

The Household and Macroeconomic Aggregates

Much of the evidence to support the thesis that household composition influences macroeconomic variables comes from the microeconomic context of the household. Authors such as Deaton (1992) argue that aggregated microeconomic data are a valid basis for forming macroeconomic conclusions. As Stotsky (2006, 8) notes, "at a disaggregate level, there is evidence to suggest that household composition may influence the full range of economic variables of choice to the household, including consumption, savings, investment, risk-taking behavior, and labor supply." Given that gender relations influence decisions made within the household, it is natural to expect to see the implications of these decisions at the macroeconomic level.

The neoclassical model traditionally treated the household as a single decision-making entity. It could therefore not deal with the fact that individual members of the household make their own decisions. As a result, individual preferences within a household were modeled separately.

In the 1960s, some economists began to view this model as outmoded and turned to new household economics (NHE). NHE brought greater flexibility to the structure of policies aimed at the household level despite the added complexity of the modeling process involved and the fact that it did not always yield policy responses. Contributed to initially by Schultz (1961, 1974) and Becker (1964, 1965), this theory treats the household as a multiple decision-making entity in which individuals make decisions to invest in both human capital (their offspring and themselves) and nonhuman capital (stocks and shares). Stotsky (2006, 8) references Strauss and Thomas (1995); Behrman (1997); Hoddinott, Alderman, and Haddad (1997); Vermeulen (2002); and Quisumbing (2003) as principal contributors to the literature showing that "household behavior does reflect the outcome of the interactions between household members with diverse preferences and resource endowments."

Figure 3.1 illustrates the gender dynamic at the level of the household, outlining the two approaches. One is a unitary model, based on a neoclassical framework in which all resources and responsibilities within the household are pooled to achieve a common set of goals. In this model, gender has no effect on savings or consumption. The second is a collective model, in which individuals within the household differ in their preferences, rights, responsibilities, and resources, as suggested by NHE models. Here two possible outcomes are noted. Where there is a pooling of resources and responsibilities, we expect no gender effects on macroeconomic variables. But if bargaining rather than cooperation characterizes household decisions—that is, if individuals within the household use the resources they control to pursue their own priorities—then policies that affect the distribution of resources within a household or shift the balance of power will have clear implications for gender equality, macroeconomics, and family welfare.

What does the evidence say about decisions at the household level? Does cooperation or bargaining hold sway? Data from the Demographic and Health Surveys (DHS) carried out by the United Nations Children's Fund (UNICEF) show that in two-thirds of the countries surveyed, less

Figure 3.1   Unitary and Collective Models of Gender Dynamic at the Household Level

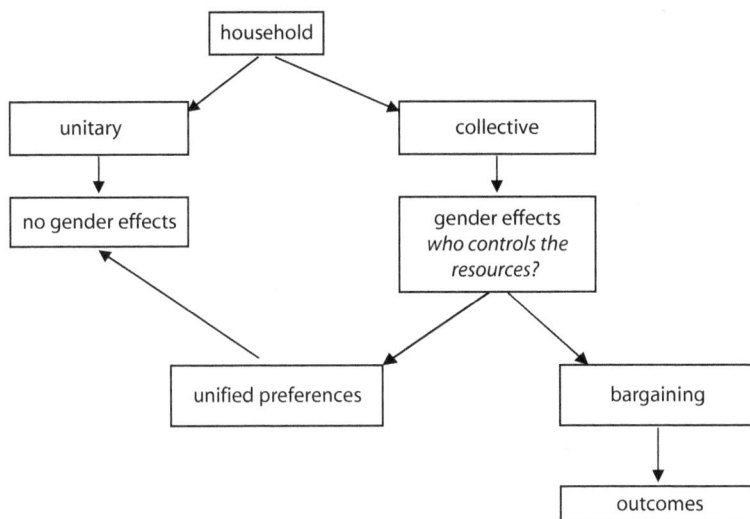

Source: Authors.

than half of the women participated in all household decisions, such as those regarding their own health care, major household purchases, daily household spending, and visits with family and relatives outside the household. Figure 3.2 examines the proportion of women who report that their husbands make decisions regarding their health.

Within the household, the person who controls the resources also controls expenditures on education, health, and nutrition. Figure 3.3 examines the proportion of women who report that their husbands alone make decisions on household spending. The shares range from a high of 65.7 percent in Malawi to a low of 2.4 percent in Indonesia.

Gender Inequalities and Consumption

Men and women frequently have very different priorities when it comes to expenditure. Studies in the 1980s suggested that men and women systematically spent money under their control in different ways (Quisumbing and McClafferty 2006).[1]

Stotsky (2006) identifies two strands of research on the effects of gender on consumption behavior. The first strand examines the fact that

Figure 3.2   Percentage of Women in Selected Countries Reporting That Their Husbands Alone Make Decisions Regarding Their Health

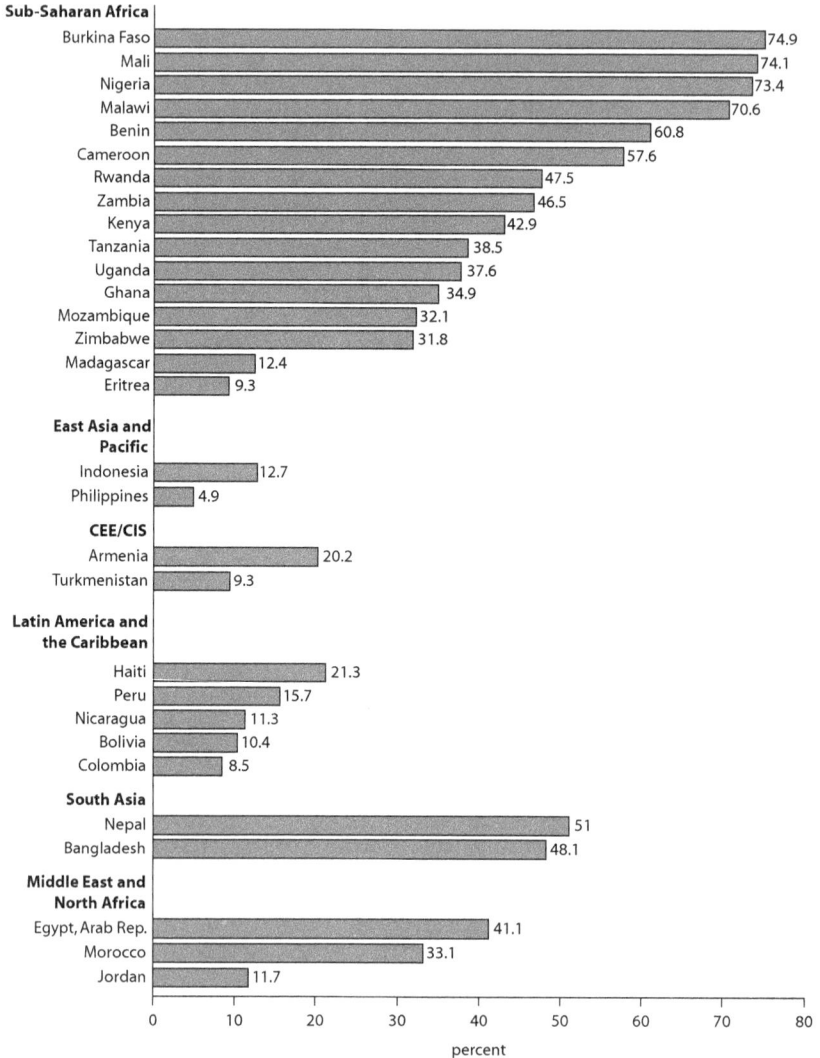

Horizontal bar chart, percent on x-axis (0 to 80).

Sub-Saharan Africa
- Burkina Faso: 74.9
- Mali: 74.1
- Nigeria: 73.4
- Malawi: 70.6
- Benin: 60.8
- Cameroon: 57.6
- Rwanda: 47.5
- Zambia: 46.5
- Kenya: 42.9
- Tanzania: 38.5
- Uganda: 37.6
- Ghana: 34.9
- Mozambique: 32.1
- Zimbabwe: 31.8
- Madagascar: 12.4
- Eritrea: 9.3

East Asia and Pacific
- Indonesia: 12.7
- Philippines: 4.9

CEE/CIS
- Armenia: 20.2
- Turkmenistan: 9.3

Latin America and the Caribbean
- Haiti: 21.3
- Peru: 15.7
- Nicaragua: 11.3
- Bolivia: 10.4
- Colombia: 8.5

South Asia
- Nepal: 51
- Bangladesh: 48.1

Middle East and North Africa
- Egypt, Arab Rep.: 41.1
- Morocco: 33.1
- Jordan: 11.7

percent

Source: UNICEF 2006, 18.
Note: Data refer to the most recent year available between 2000 and 2004. All countries for which data were available are presented. CEE/CIS = Central and Eastern Europe/Commonwealth of Independent States.

women have a stronger preference than men for spending on goods and services that contribute to the human capital of their children. This difference implies that households in which women control the resources will spend more on education, health, and nutrition. Quisumbing and McClafferty (2006, 11) note that "the most consistent effect across

Figure 3.3   Percentage of Women in Selected Countries Reporting That Their Husbands Alone Make Decisions on Daily Household Expenditures

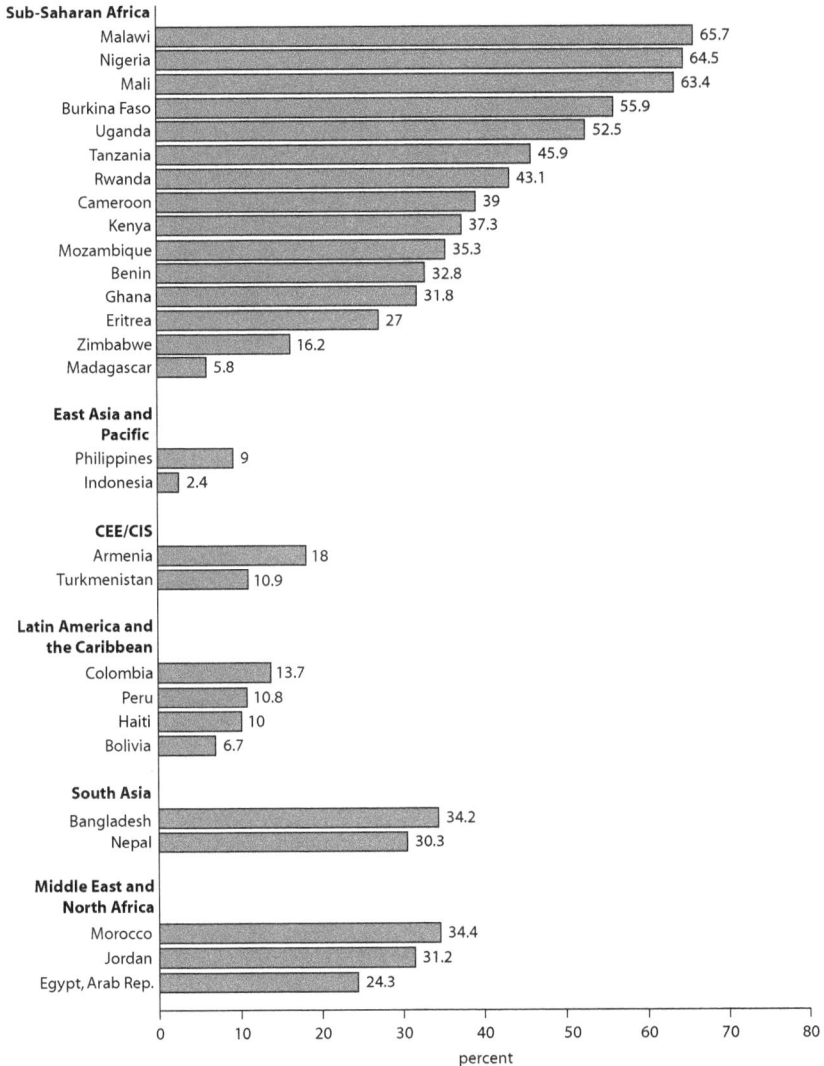

Source: UNICEF 2006, 19.
Note: Data refer to the most recent year available between 2000 and 2004. All countries for which data were available are presented. CEE/CIS = Central and Eastern Europe/Commonwealth of Independent States.

countries is that resources controlled by women tend to increase expenditure shares on education relative to resources controlled by men." Table 3.1 summarizes some of the other findings from the literature on the effect of gender effects on household consumption.

Table 3.1   Gender Effects on Household Consumption Behavior

Study	Household situation examined	Region or country	Effects on household consumption
Blumberg (1988)	Differences in share of resources controlled by men and women	Latin America, North Africa, Sub-Saharan Africa, South Asia	Women spend less on themselves, more on their children, more on family's basic needs.
Bruce (1989)	Effect of greater influence by women over household spending	Kerala, India	Nutritional status of children is directly related to mother's income.
Quisumbing and Maluccio (2003)	Effects of bargaining power (based on resources brought to marriage by women and men) on expenditures on food, education, health, children's clothing, and alcohol or tobacco	Bangladesh, Ethiopia, Indonesia, South Africa	Bargaining power has different effects on shares spent on education in all countries; whether boys or girls benefit depends on the country.
Thomas (1997)	Effect of additional income to the household versus additional income to women	Brazil	Additional income benefits children regardless of gender, but women's spending is more beneficial to children's survival and nutrition than men's.

Source: Authors' compilation based on Stotsky 2006, 9–10.

A number of studies show that increasing a woman's decision-making power within the household increases spending on education, health, and nutrition (table 3.2 draws on some of this research). Quisumbing and McClafferty (2006) offer a nontechnical presentation of the findings from the International Food Policy Research Institute's (IFPRI's) multi-country research program on gender and intrahousehold issues, along with implications and key questions for integrating gender research findings into project cycle and policy decision-making processes.

Gender differences in spending have clear implications for the macroeconomy and for macroeconomic policy. Stotsky (2006, 11) notes the macroeconomic implications of women's tendency to spend more on necessities than men do:

• Greater spending on goods and services that increase human capital will ultimately affect economic growth.

Table 3.2   Effects on Consumption of Increasing Decision-Making Power by Women

Study	Region or country	Input variables	Output variables	Outcome
Hallman (2000)	Bangladesh	Women's asset holdings	Women's health	The higher the share of women's asset holdings, the better the health outcome for girls.
Quisumbing (1996)	Sub-Saharan Africa	Human capital Physical capital Current inputs	Agricultural productivity	Reducing gender inequalities in human capital, physical capital, and current inputs has the potential to increase agricultural productivity by 10–20 percent.
Quisumbing and Maluccio (2000)	Not specified	Women's asset holdings at marriage	Children's education	The larger the share of assets women hold at marriage, the larger the share the household spends on children's education.
Smith and Chavas (2003)	Not specified	Women's decision making within society and family	Child nutrition	Improvements in women's decision-making power significantly reduce child malnutrition rates.

Source: Authors' compilation.

- Given that necessities remain constant regardless of variations in income, one would expect more stable expenditure in economies in which women have a greater degree of control over household purchases.
- Policies that improve women's control over household spending should strengthen macroeconomic growth and stability.

The second strand of the literature referenced by Stotsky (2006) examines the fact that the gender of children in some cultures determines the amount of expenditure they receive. At the individual level, gender affects consumption of education, health, and nutrition. For example, Schultz (1987) shows that in 90 countries, an increase in the cost of schooling or a decrease in household income decreases girls' consumption of education (both primary and secondary school enrollment rates and total years of schooling) more than boys' consumption. In India, Kingdon (2005) finds gender bias in the allocation of spending on education for boys. In fact, households are unlikely to pay for any education for girls.

Deaton (1989) finds no gender bias in medical and education spending in Côte d'Ivoire and only a small but insignificant effect in favor of boys in Thailand. Across several developing countries, Glick, Saha, and Younger (2004) find no discrimination in health care or education spending among boys and girls in their review of the literature and analyses of developing country data sets. Alderman and Gertler (1997) find a gender bias in favor of boys with regard to demand for medical care in Pakistan.

Lewis and Lockheed (2007) illustrate the extent and degree of the problem of girls' exclusion from formal education:

- In India 37 percent of girls 7–14 belonging to lower castes or tribes do not attend school, compared with 26 percent of all girls the same age; school attendance for tribal girls is 9 percentage points less than that of tribal boys.
- In the Lao People's Democratic Republic hill tribe girls from rural communities complete less than two years of school, whereas majority Lao-Tai girls from urban communities complete eight years.
- In Guatemala indigenous girls are less likely than any other group of children to have ever enrolled in primary school: only 26 percent of indigenous non-Spanish-speaking girls complete primary school, compared with 62 percent of Spanish-speaking girls.
- In the Slovak Republic, only 9 percent of Roma girls attend secondary school, compared with 54 percent of Slovak girls.

Macroeconomic policy that targets the exclusion of girls from education needs to consider the price and income elasticities of demand for education. As Stotsky (2006) notes, relative price increases for education would adversely affect girls, and price decreases would disproportionately benefit girls: "Higher income elasticity of demand for female education and health care implies that economic prosperity would disproportionately benefit women by expanding their access to these services, while recessions would have a disproportionately negative effect" (Stotsky 2006, 11). Sound macroeconomic policies that include an appropriately valued exchange rate are key to reducing gender disparities in education and health.[2]

Lewis and Lockheed (2007) suggest two avenues by which policy can "reach and teach" excluded girls. The first avenue involves improving the quality and accessibility of education in the following ways:

- *Make education policies fairer.* Some policies—such as the requirement that lessons be taught in the majority language—have unintentional consequences. In some cases, girls from an excluded group will not have had the same exposure to majority languages as boys. Policies that require single-sex schooling or coeducation may also limit girls' opportunities. The authors cite the example of areas in Pakistan where only boys' schools have been established and where some parents do not allow older girls to attend coeducational schools.

- *Expand schooling options.* Schooling options may be expanded for excluded groups, particularly girls, in a number of ways. In Bolivia, Brazil, India, and Turkey, preschool programs help excluded groups make the transition to formal schooling. A community in Rajasthan, India, selected and supervised teachers for preschool programs and hired part-time workers to escort girls from excluded groups to school. Radio, television, and computers also expand opportunities for excluded groups, especially girls who stay at home after primary school.

- *Improve the physical environment and instructional materials.* School quality—infrastructure, absentee rates among teachers, and school supplies—matters more for excluded groups than for children from mainstream families. Minority parents often have higher expectations of school quality.

The second avenue creates incentives for households to send girls to school. Although Lewis and Lockheed (2007, 19) note that "evidence on what incentives might work is less clear and needs more focused evaluation," they propose several promising options:

- *Offer conditional cash transfers.* Transfers help households defray some of the costs of education, although such programs are often difficult to administer. Programs in Bangladesh, Ecuador, and Mexico have been successful, although their impact on excluded groups has not been assessed.

- *Offer scholarships and stipends for girls.* Offering scholarships and stipends for girls to stay in school after the primary level is based on the same principle as offering transfers. Such incentives have been very effective in many countries, especially Bangladesh, where student enrollment increased to twice the national average for girls in districts that offered such incentives. In fact, the mere existence of an opportunity to earn a scholarship improved enrollment.

- *Introduce school feeding programs.* School feeding programs have been shown to boost enrollment and attendance, although they do little to reduce the gender gap. Indeed, studies show that boys benefit more than girls from such programs.

Lampietti and Stalker (2000) examine consumption expenditure and female poverty. Referencing more than 60 poverty assessments carried out by the World Bank and other published and unpublished sources, the authors note the following:

- Poor women have higher fertility rates, higher maternal mortality rates, lower-birthweight babies, and less access to qualified or modern health care during pregnancy than nonpoor women do. These differences are found in both low- and middle-income countries.
- There is no conclusive evidence that poor women are worse off than poor men in terms of food allocation and anthropometric status (a measure of food intakes).
- Low- and middle-income countries vary in the quantity and kind of educational opportunities they offer boys and girls. Several findings emerge from analysis of 22 poverty assessments that included analysis of gender and education. Girls are worse off than boys in Djibouti, Egypt, Kenya, Nigeria, Pakistan, and Yemen. Below the poverty line, girls are worse off than boys in Algeria, Bolivia, Côte d'Ivoire, India, Lao PDR, Malawi, Morocco, and Zambia; boys are worse off than girls in Lesotho and Mongolia. The findings are inconclusive or show no difference in Madagascar, Mauritania, Nicaragua, Rwanda, Sri Lanka, and Tanzania.

Gender Inequalities and Savings

Stotsky (2006) notes that gender relations may affect savings behavior, almost certainly at the level of the household but also domestically and internationally and with regard to preferences for risk taking. At the level of the economy, gender-based differences influence domestic savings, with implications for investment and economic growth. Furthermore, investment behavior arising from gender-based differences in savings may have implications for exports and imports.

Stotsky (2006) reviews the literature on savings and gender, highlighting the reasons why people in developing economies may have different motivations to save than people in developed economies. In developed economies, savings help smooth consumption over the life cycle and fulfill bequest, investment, and precautionary motives (Stotsky 2006).

Agenor and Montiel (1996) and Gerosvitz (1989) suggest reasons why these motivations may not hold as strongly in developing economies:

- Households in developing countries are organized differently from households in developed countries and usually incorporate a large extended family. This difference could increase savings to facilitate intergenerational well-being, but it could also reduce savings, as individuals may choose not to save for retirement but rely instead on income from the next generation.
- There is less potential for consumption in developing countries, because most households are at or below the subsistence level.
- Household income may vary significantly over time, making savings behavior less certain.
- Lack of or a low level of savings limits households' ability to borrow.

Seguino and Floro (2003) examine the differences in savings behavior between men and women in developing economies. As summarized in Stotsky (2006), they suggest a number of reasons why women may have a greater incentive than men to save:

- A woman's role as a homemaker suggests that she has a greater incentive to save for consumption-smoothing purposes than men, who have access to social insurance (such as unemployment benefits) through paid employment.
- Women are more likely to save for life-cycle purposes, given their greater longevity.
- Women may have stronger bequest motives and intergenerational altruism, which may make them more likely to save for their heirs.

Women in some areas face greater constraints than men in participating in formal financial markets, potentially affecting their ability to save. Thus, in some contexts, women save outside of formal markets. In other contexts, such as Bangladesh, women save less, because they are required to hand over their savings to male household members (Goetz and Gupta 1996).

Although most studies on gender-based differences in savings examine developed economies, they nevertheless reveal differences in savings and investment behavior based on gender.[3] Using data on aggregate savings ratios from a group of semi-industrial countries over the period 1975–95, Seguino and Floro (2003) find that women's wage share relative to men's is positive and significantly related to savings. Floro (2001) notes that poor women have a greater propensity to save than men do.

Conclusion

It is now generally accepted that women have a stronger preference than men for spending on goods and services that increase the human capital of their children. The macroeconomic implications of this statement are clear. Greater expenditure and investment in human capital will ultimately influence economic growth. Furthermore, expenditure on services such as education, health, and nutrition is less responsive to variations in income, thus bringing about greater stability in expenditure in economies in which women have greater control over household purchases. Policies that increase women's control of household spending should therefore strengthen macroeconomic growth. At the individual level, gender affects consumption of education, health, and nutrition. A number of studies attest to the discrimination faced by women and girls in education. The chapter examines some policies that could increase parity in education for women and girls in developing countries.

The chapter reviewed the evidence on gender inequalities in savings behavior, noting that the lack of data from developing countries makes it difficult to draw firm conclusions. A number of studies examine why savings rates may be different in developed and developing economies, paying special attention to who controls the resources in the household. Some evidence suggests that men and women exhibit different savings behavior, with women more likely than men to save for consumption-smoothing purposes, to make bequests to their children, and to ensure income for their longer lives.

Notes

1. Quisumbing and McClafferty (2006) cite studies by Guyer (1980), Tripp (1982), Pahl (1983), and Fapohunda (1988), all of which are discussed in Dwyer and Bruce (1988).

2. An overvalued exchange rate could raise the price of domestic goods and services, including education.

3. Lack of appropriate savings data in developing economies hampers further study.

Bibliography

Agenor, P. R., and P. J. Montiel. 1996. *Development Macroeconomics.* Princeton, NJ: Princeton University Press.

Alderman, H., and P. Gertler. 1997. "Family Resources and Gender Differences in Human Capital Investments: The Demand for Children's Medical Care in Pakistan." In *Intrahousehold Resource Allocation in Developing Countries,* ed. L. Haddad, J. Hoddinott, and H. Alderman, 231–48. Baltimore, MD: Johns Hopkins University Press.

Becker, G. 1964. *Human Capital.* New York: Columbia University Press.

———. 1965. "A Theory of the Allocation of Time." *Economic Journal* 75 (299): 493–517.

Behrman, J. 1997. "Intrahousehold Distribution and the Family." In *Handbook of Population and Family Economics,* vol. 1A, ed. M. R. Rosenzweig and O. Stark, 125–87. Amsterdam: Elsevier Science.

Blumberg, R. L. 1988. "Income under Female versus Male Control: Hypothesis from a Theory of Gender Stratification and Data from the Third World." *Journal of Family Issues* 9: 51–84.

Bruce, J. 1989. "Homes Divided." *World Development* 17 (7): 97–91.

Case, A., and A. Deaton. 2003. "Consumption, Health, Gender and Poverty." Policy Research Working Paper 3020, World Bank, Poverty Reduction and Economic Management, Gender and Development, Washington, DC.

Deaton, A. 1989. "Looking for Boy-Girl Discrimination in Household Expenditure Data." *World Bank Economic Review* 3 (1): 1–15.

———. 1992. *Understanding Consumption.* Oxford: Oxford University Press.

Dwyer, D., and J. Bruce, eds. 1988. *A Home Divided: Women and Income in the Third World.* Stanford, CA: Stanford University Press.

Fapohunda, E. 1988. "The Nonpooling Household: A Challenge to Theory." In *A Home Divided: Women and Income in the Third World,* ed. D. Dwyer and J. Bruce. Stanford, CA: Stanford University Press.

Floro, M. S. 2001. "Gender Dimensions of the Financing for Development Agenda." Working Paper prepared for the United Nations Development Fund for Women, United Nations, New York.

Gerosvitz, M. 1989. "Saving and Development." In *Handbook of Development Economics,* ed. H. Chenery and T. N. Srinivasan, vol. 1A, 382–424. Amsterdam: Elsevier Science.

Glick, P., R. Saha, and S. D. Younger. 2004. "Integrating Gender into Benefit Incidence and Demand Analysis." Cornell University Food and Nutrition Policy Program, Ithaca, NY.

Goetz, A. M., and R. S. Gupta. 1996. "Who Takes the Credit? Gender, Power, and Control over Loan Use in Rural Credit Programs in Bangladesh." *World Development* 24 (2): 45–63.

Guyer, J. M. 1980. "Household Budgets and Women's Incomes." African Studies Center Working Paper No. 28, Boston University, Boston, MA.

Hallman, H. K. 2000. "Mother-Father Resource Control, Marriage Payments and Girl-Boy Health in Rural Bangladesh." Food Consumption and Nutrition Division (FCND) Discussion Paper 93, International Food Policy Research Institute (IFPRI), Washington, DC.

Hoddinott, J., H. Alderman, and L. Haddad. 1997. "Testing Competing Models of Intrahousehold Allocation." In *Intrahousehold Resource Allocation in Developing Countries*, ed. L. Haddad, J. Hoddinott, and H. Alderman, 129–41. Baltimore, MD: Johns Hopkins University Press.

Jackson, C. 2005. "Strengthening Food Policy through Gender and Intrahousehold Analysis: Impact Assessment of IFPRI Multicountry Research." IFPRI Impact Assessment Discussion Paper 23, International Food Policy Research Institute, Washington, DC.

Kingdon, G. G. 2005. "Where Has All the Bias Gone? Detecting Gender Bias in the Intrahousehold Allocation of Educational Expenditure." *Economic Development and Cultural Change* 53 (2): 409–51.

Lampietti, J. A., and L. Stalker. 2000. "Consumption Expenditure and Female Poverty: A Review of the Evidence." Policy Research Report on Gender and Development, Working Paper Series 11, World Bank, Washington, DC.

Lewis, M. A., and M. E. Lockheed. 2007. "Getting All Girls into School." *Finance and Development* 44 (2): 16–19.

Pahl, J. 1983. "The Allocation of Money within Marriage." *Sociological Review* 32 (May): 237–64.

Quisumbing, A. R., ed. 1996. "Male-Female Differences in Agricultural Productivity: Methodological Issues and Empirical Evidence." *World Development Report* 24 (10): 1575–95.

———. 2003. *Household Decisions, Gender and Development: A Synthesis of Recent Research.* International Food Policy Research Institute (IFPRI), Washington, DC.

———. 2006. *Using Gender Research in Development.* International Food Policy Research Institute (IFPRI), Washington, DC.

Quisumbing, A. R., and J. A. Maluccio. 2000. "Intrahousehold Allocation and Gender Relations: New Empirical Evidence from Four Developing Countries." FCND Discussion Paper 84, International Food Policy Research Institute, Washington, DC.

———. 2003. "Resources at Marriage and Intrahousehold Allocation: Evidence from Bangladesh, Ethiopia, Indonesia and South Africa." *Oxford Bulletin of Economics and Statistics* 65 (3): 283–327.

Quisumbing, A. R., and B. McClafferty. 2006. *Using Gender Research in Development. Food Security in Practice.* International Food Policy Research Institute (IFPRI), Washington, DC.

Schultz, T. P. 1961. "Investments in Human Capital." *American Economic Review* 51 (1): 1–17.

———. 1974. *Economics of the Family, Marriage, Children and Human Capital.* Chicago: Chicago University Press.

———. 1987. "School Expenditures and Enrollments, 1960–1980: The Effects of Income, Prices and Population Growth." In *Population Growth and Economic Development: Issues and Evidence,* ed. D. Gale Johnson and R. D. Lee, 413–76. Madison: University of Wisconsin Press.

Seguino, S., and M. S. Floro. 2003. "Does Gender Have Any Effect on Aggregate Saving: An Empirical Analysis." *International Review of Applied Economics* 17 (2): 147–66.

Smith, L. C., and J-P. Chavas. 2003. "Supply Response of West African Agricultural Households: Implications of Intrahousehold Preference Heterogeneity." In *Households, Decisions, Gender and Development: A Synthesis of Recent Research,* ed. A. R. Quisumbing. Washington, DC: IFPRI.

Stotsky, J. 2006. "Gender and Its Relevance to Macroeconomic Policy: A Survey." IMF Working Paper WP/06/233, International Monetary Fund, Washington, DC.

Strauss, J., and D. Thomas. 1995. "Human Resources: Empirical Modeling of Household and Family Decisions." In *Handbook of Development Economics,* ed. J. Behrman and T. N. Srinivasan, (3A), 1882–2023. New York: North Holland.

Thomas, D. 1997. "Incomes, Expenditures and Health Outcomes: Evidence on Intrahousehold Resource Allocation." In *Intrahousehold Resource Allocation in Developing Countries,* ed. L. Haddad, J. Hoddinott, and H. Alderman, 142–64. Baltimore, MD: Johns Hopkins University Press.

Tripp, R. 1982. "Farmers and Traders: Some Economic Determinants of Nutritional Status in Northern Ghana." *Food and Nutrition Bulletin* 8 (1): 3–12.

UNICEF (United Nations Children's Fund). 2006. *The State of the World's Children 2007. Women and Children: The Double Dividend of Gender Equality.* New York: UNICEF.

Vermeulen, F. 2002. "Collective Household Models: Principles and Main Results." *Journal of Economic Surveys* 16 (4): 1869–80.

CHAPTER 4

Gender and Economic Growth

Developments in growth theory in recent decades facilitate a much broader interpretation of the factors contributing to economic growth, including gender relations. This chapter explores gender relations and economic growth, examining the statistical evidence and theoretical literature from both the growth-theory and feminist perspectives. Empirical studies are then analyzed in light of the statistical relationships and theoretical frameworks. The chapter concludes by considering how economic growth affects gender inequalities.

Based on what we know about gender and economics, we expect to see a reciprocal relationship between gender inequality and economic growth. Stotsky (2006, 17) states that "gender disparities lead to weaker economic growth and that stronger economic growth leads to reduced gender disparities," adding that growth may affect gender inequalities by breaking down barriers to women's work participation, reducing the time spent in the home on nonmarket labor, and changing institutional mores.

Statistical Relationships

A number of measures of gender equality are positively correlated with economic growth, as measured by per capita income (table 4.1). Although

Table 4.1   Indicators of Gender Equality and Relationships with Per Capita Income

Indicator	Relationship with log of per capita income	Comments
Ratio of girls to boys in primary education	Flat relationship with clear outliers	Suggests no (statistical) impact on gender equality.
Ratio of girls to boys in secondary education	Slightly negative relationship	Suggests some improvement of low-income countries in female education, thus resulting in higher ratios in the lower-income countries.
Life expectancy	Positive but scattered	Given that women live, on average, six years longer than men in developed nations, a positive relationship implies that as income rises, women are more likely to achieve the biological norm in relative life expectancy
Fertility	Negative but scattered	Higher fertility is usually associated with lower gender equality and lower income.

Source: Stotsky 2006, 22.

this relationship does not imply causality, it suggests variables that may be used in regression analysis to determine the presence or absence of a statistically significant relationship that, in turn, may be used to inform policy. Stotsky (2006) separately plots both the UN Gender-related Development Index (GDI) and the Gender Empowerment Measure (GEM) against the log of per capita income for 41 countries chosen randomly from the sample of International Monetary Fund (IMF) member countries. Both indexes show positive and nonlinear relationships with income, suggesting that increasing income leads to greater gender equality in both economic terms (as measured by the GDI) and political terms (as measured by the GEM) (figure 4.1).

Several studies examine the empirical relationship between single indicators of gender equality and per capita income. Stotsky (2006) examines the relationship between the log of per capita income and the ratio of girls to boys in primary education, the ratio in secondary education, and life expectancy (see her paper for the list of countries and detailed results). She concludes that the relationship between single indicators of gender equality and per capita income is less clear than the relationship between income and indexes such as the GEM and GDI.

Dollar and Gatti (1999) also examine correlations between gender measures and per capita income, using data from 80 developing countries

Figure 4.1   Gender-Related Development Index (GDI) and Gender Empowerment Measure (GEM) versus Per Capita Gross Domestic Product (GDP) in Selected Countries, 2002

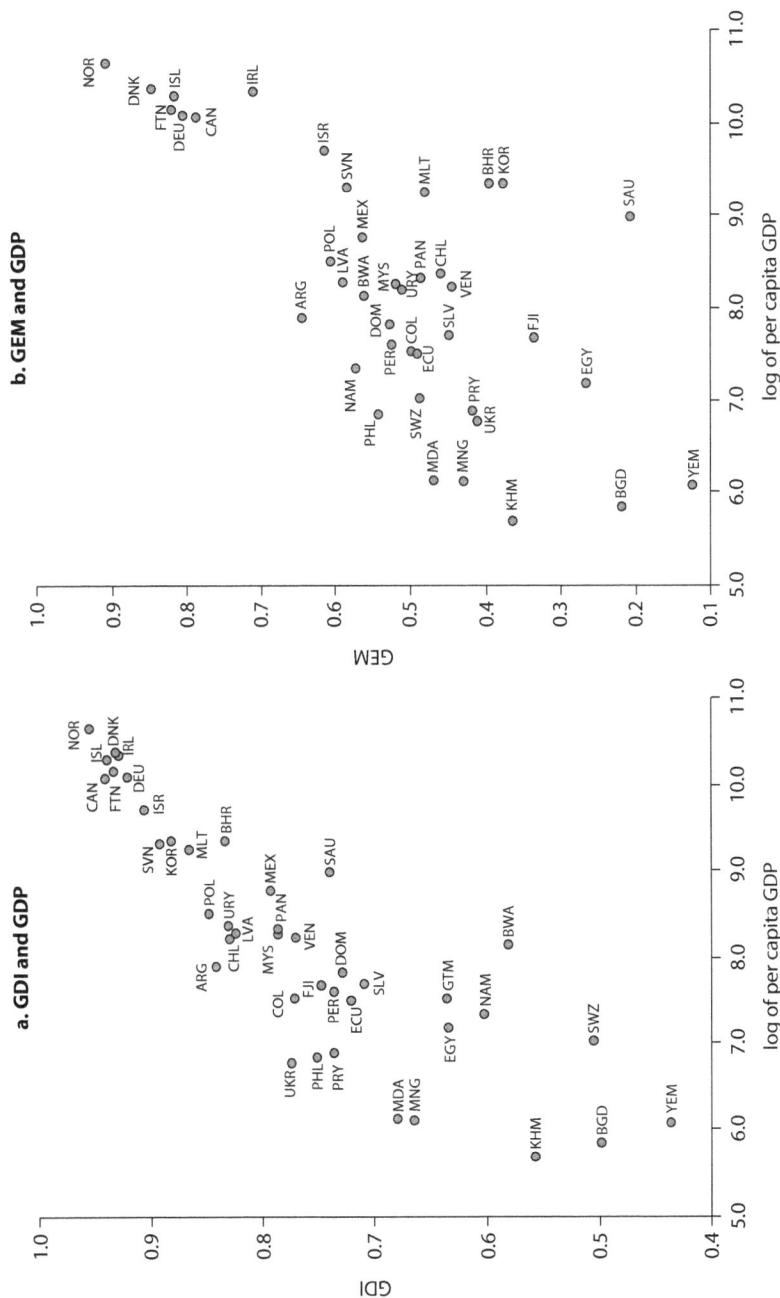

a. GDI and GDP

b. GEM and GDP

Source: Stotsky 2006, 23–24.

Note: Every third member of the IMF in alphabetical order was chosen; if no data were available, the next country on the list was chosen.

67

Table 4.2   Correlations between Gender Measures and Per Capita Income in 80 Developing Countries, 1990

Measure	Income	Secondary education	Life expectancy	Economic rights	Marriage rights
Per capita income					
Secondary education differential	0.28				
Life expectancy differential	0.61	0.35			
Women's economic rights	0.60	0.20	0.58		
Women's marriage rights	0.64	0.28	0.71	0.66	
Women in parliament	0.43	−0.05	0.27	0.40	0.43

Source: Dollar and Gatti 1999, 26.

(table 4.2). All measures of gender equality are positively correlated with per capita income, ranging from 28 percent for gender differences in secondary education to about 60 percent for women's life expectancy minus men's life expectancy, women's economic rights (equal pay for equal work), and women's rights within marriage.

Comparing the poorest and richest countries using 1990 per capita income data reveals striking differences (table 4.3). For example, just 5.4 percent of young women in the lowest-quartile countries have some higher education, compared with 11.6 percent of young men. The contrast with the richest quartile is even starker: gender difference has been largely eliminated—50.8 percent of women and 57.9 percent of men have some higher education. Differences in life expectancy between men and women are relatively small in the poorest quartile—roughly three years on average compared with six years in the richest countries. Based on a scale of 1 to 4 developed by Humana (1992) to measure a variety of rights, economic rights for women in the poorest countries average 2.0, compared with 2.9 in the richest countries. Women's rights within marriage average 2.3 in the poorest countries, compared with 3.6 in the richest countries. In the poorest countries, women hold just 7 percent of seats in the lower house of parliament, compared with 17 percent in the richest countries, and the median year in which women were granted the right to vote is 36 years later (Dollar and Gatti 1999).

Theoretical Considerations

The theoretical literature, in particular the literature from the neoclassical approach and the feminist viewpoint, explores the relationship between

Table 4.3   Gender Indicators in Poorest and Richest Quartiles of Countries, 1990

Indicator	Poorest quartile	Richest quartile
Secondary attainment		
Female	5.0	37.7
Male	10.4	38.7
Postsecondary attainment		
Female	5.4	50.8
Male	11.6	57.9
Life expectancy		
Female	51.3	79.1
Male	48.3	73.0
Women's rights		
Economic rights (1–4)	2.0	2.9
Marriage rights (1–4)	2.3	3.6
Women's political power		
Percentage of seats held in lower house of parliament	7	17
Year women granted right to vote	1962	1926

Source: Dollar and Gatti 1999, 26.
Note: The poorest quartile includes countries in which annual per capita income was $1,182 or less. The richest quartile includes countries in which annual per capita income was $7,478 or more.

gender inequality and economic growth. Forsythe, Korzeniewicz, and Durrant (2000) categorize the literature on the ways in which economic growth affects gender inequalities into three perspectives: neoclassical/modernization, Boserup/women in development (WID), and gender and development (GAD). To this we would add endogenous growth theory, which can accommodate gender disparities (table 4.4).

The neoclassical/modernization approach has its roots in neoclassical theory, which relates economic growth to capital accumulation and savings, which in turn depend on the distribution of resources, income, and capabilities. As previous chapters have shown, gender inequalities affect these inputs at the microeconomic level; gender inequalities can therefore affect economic growth at the aggregate level.[1] As Stotsky (2006, 18) notes, "the neoclassical approach examines the simultaneous interaction of economic development and the reduction of gender inequalities. It sees the process of economic development leading to the reduction of these inequalities and also inequalities hindering economic development."

The neoclassical/modernization approach suggests that gender inequalities resulting from disparities in human capital are likely to diminish as the economy grows. Forsythe, Korzeniewicz, and Durrant (2000) argue that gender inequality in employment, wages, and vulnerability to poverty stems from gender-based differences in education, skills, and expected

Table 4.4   Theses and Outcomes of Four Perspectives on Economic Growth and Gender Inequalities

Growth perspective	Thesis	Outcome for gender inequalities
Neoclassical/ modernization	Economic growth promotes greater equality between men and women.	Growth and development reduce gender inequalities. Inequality between men and women will decline following improvements in selected measures of women's status.
Boserup/women in development (WID)	Policy makers must intervene to correct gender biases before growth will promote equality.	
Gender and development (GAD)	Growth has a complicated effect on gender equality.	Improvements in selected measures of women's status cannot be assumed to translate into reductions in inequalities; such inequalities may remain or even become entrenched.
Endogenous growth	By including human capital, endogenous growth theory paves the way for considering produced and reproduced labor inputs.	Given that women are more likely than men to invest in children, the gender distribution of income could affect growth (Stotsky 2006, 18).

Source: Authors' compilation, based on Forsythe, Korzeniewicz, and Durrant 2000.

length of labor force participation. They believe that economic expansion will undermine gender discrimination in labor markets and social capital in the long run.[2]

Discriminatory social mores and norms may change in the long run as well, improving gender equality—or they may remain intact, working against economic modernization and growth to maintain inequality. For example, some observers maintain that "enduring patriarchal institutions will prevent gender equality even in the face of economic advancement" (Jütting and others 2006, 7, citing Marchand and Parpart 1995 and Parpart 1993). They point to Saudi Arabia—a high-income country with poor gender equality—as evidence. Others, such as Ramirez, Soysal, and Shanahan (1997), suggest that even in societies with strong patriarchal institutional legacies, there is some evidence that globalization has displaced traditional gender inequalities.

Boserup (1970) advances an alternative view, arguing that economic growth in the initial stages of development is characterized by a widening gap between men and women, represented by a curvilinear relationship between economic growth and the status of women.[3] Productivity differences between men and women at low levels of economic development are relatively minor; as development progresses, productivity differences widen and a "polarization and hierarchization of men and women's work roles ensue" (Forsythe, Korzeniewicz, and Durrant 2000, 575). Roles become entrenched and possibly propagated by discrimination, which further influences the organization of the labor market. Two outcomes are possible.

First, assuming further economic development, the gap begins to close or at least ceases to widen, as under the neoclassical approach. Forsythe, Korzeniewicz, and Durrant (2000) point to the tight labor markets and increasing demand for female workers that would arise if women were continuously excluded from wage activities. The authors also show that as economies develop, policy makers eventually create greater opportunities for women in education and training, accompanied by higher rates of labor force participation among women. Finally, "with development, women seek to acquire greater bargaining power in their families," for example, by being "better able to support themselves if their husbands desert them or treat them badly" (Forsythe, Korzeniewicz, and Durrant 2000, 576).

Second, cultural traditions play a key role in influencing women's decisions to take part in the labor force. Boserup (1970, 97) notes that "cultural traditions, including the role of women in the traditional sector of market trade, seem to be a more important factor in determining the place of women in the modern trade sector than is the stage of general 'modernization' achieved by the country."

In recent decades, Boserup's analysis has shaped development policy and advocacy related to women. As Forsythe, Korzeniewicz, and Durrant (2000) note, Boserup's argument highlighted the hidden contribution of women to development, called for policy makers to become more sensitive to the importance of nonmarket activities, and identified women as crucial actors who shape the success or failure of alternative development strategies

Boserup's analysis also catalyzed the WID approach, which focuses on determining the impact of development strategies on women and gender inequalities and the overall success of the development effort. The World Bank has acknowledged the WID approach as an important component of its developmental efforts.

Critical feminism and the GAD approach focus on the continuing or rising vulnerability of women over the course of economic development. They generally oppose the previous two approaches. The GAD approach has been used to critique the WID approach, denouncing it as a top-down strategy that ignores the particularities of gender inequality. According to this argument, policies that draw from aggregate data to improve the status of women treat gender inequality as a homogeneous field, thus failing to take into account its different effects on different groups of people. By ignoring these subtleties, this top-down approach may actually exacerbate inequalities and create new problems. For example, teenage girls in low-income households were more likely than teenage boys to see their educational opportunities curtailed following a period of structural adjustment (Agarwal 1974; Bandarage 1984; Staundt 1985; Moser 1993; Kabeer 1994; and Elson 1995, all cited in Forsythe, Korzeniewicz, and Durrant 2000).

The relationship between the economic and social position of women and gender equality is central to the GAD theory. Do improvements in the status of women improve gender equality, or are the two concepts independent of each other? Some theorists suggest that economic and social measures such as income and education are insufficient to determine women's status (Kabeer 1994). Moore and Shackman (1996) conclude that "neither high levels of economic prosperity nor development of women's 'human capital' through education and employment necessarily result in increased access to authority positions for women" (cited in Forsythe, Korzeniewcz, and Durrant 2000, 578). Nuss and Majka (1983) note that improvements in educational attainment or decisions about fertility do not directly translate into improvements in women's status.

Forsythe, Korzeniewicz, and Durrant (2000) identify two tenets of the GAD literature: (a) that economic development has no effect on gender inequalities and (b) that economic development actually exacerbates these differences. Proponents of the first tenet argue that gender inequalities are so entrenched in patriarchal family structures, discriminatory labor practices, and property laws that they are resistant to economic growth and development. Youssef (1972), Benería (1982), and Folbre (1986) suggest that in certain regions, gender inequalities provide greater insight into labor force participation than economic development does. Semyonov (1980) notes that sex discrimination within the household is more likely in areas with entrenched gender inequalities. Draper (1985) writes that educational gains by women have no impact on labor discrimination in societies marked by gender inequalities.

Some writers take the argument one step farther, suggesting that economic growth exacerbates inequalities. Tinker (1976) maintains that inequalities are so entrenched that economic growth exacerbates the income gap between men and women, perpetuating gender inequality. Ward (1984) asserts that globalization has reduced women's status relative to men.

The GAD approach has been central to the criticisms of the structural adjustment programs administered by international financial institutions in debt-plagued countries. These criticisms have focused on the failure of these programs to account for adverse effects on certain vulnerable groups, most notably women, who are disproportionately poor and disempowered (see Afshar and Dennis 1992; Elson 1995; and Emeagwali 1995). Buchman (1996), noting that young women in particular suffer, shows that teenage girls from low-income households are less likely to enroll in secondary school than teenage boys from similar backgrounds. In contrast to these negative short-run effects, women would likely benefit from structural adjustment programs in the long run if such programs succeed in spurring growth and reducing poverty (see Lele 1986; Sparr 1994; Killick 1995; and Lantican, Gladwin, and Seale 1996, all cited in Forsythe, Korzeniewicz, and Durrant 2000, 579).

Endogenous growth theory provides a fourth framework for analyzing the effects of gender inequalities on economic growth.[4] This theory facilitates a broader interpretation of labor, one that encompasses education and training.

According to Walters (1995), the inclusion of the human capital element in endogenous growth theory paves the way for a consideration of gender in four ways:[5]

- It opens the way for time to be incorporated into the production of labor inputs.
- It recognizes education and other influences on human capital accumulation and their relationship to growth.
- It allows for the possibility of trade-offs between government fiscal policies, including spending programs, and growth.
- It facilitates income distribution through the positive effect of human capital investment on growth.

Other researchers have focused on the long-term impact of fertility on growth in endogenous growth theory. Galor and Weil (1996) incorporate fertility and its link to economic growth in their theoretical model, which shows that when wages are endogenously determined, an increase in capital per worker raises women's relative wages, which reduces fertility and thus further raises capital per worker. This virtuous cycle leads to a rapid transition to lower fertility and higher output growth.

Empirical Studies

Correctly specified econometric models can provide valuable insights into the complex relationship between gender equality and economic growth. Although the reciprocal relationship between the two makes it difficult to fully isolate the effects of either one, a variety of estimation techniques offer solutions. Many of these technique—for example, the two-stage least squares method—depend on rich sources of data that may not be available, especially in developing economies. They will become increasingly useful as these data become available.

The results from the empirical studies fall into three categories. A number of studies show a positive relationship between gender equality and economic growth, suggesting a win-win scenario: improving gender equality improves growth and vice versa. At the other end of the spectrum are studies that posit a positive relationship between gender inequality and economic growth, a lose-win scenario. In between are studies that examine facets of gender discrimination that act as a brake on economic growth; once these problems are remedied, economic growth ensues. It is not surprising that such a classification exists: gender relations rely on social norms and conventions as well as economic factors and are subject to change over time. We examine an empirical study from each scenario below.

Dollar and Gatti (1999) conclude that gender equality and economic growth are mutually reinforcing: "Societies that have a preference for not investing in girls pay a price for it in terms of slower growth and reduced income" (Dollar and Gatti 1999, 1). The authors present a win-win scenario for gender inequality and growth: reduce gender inequality, improve growth. Using data from more than 100 countries over three decades, they investigate the relationships among gender inequality, income, and growth. They note that only 5 percent of adult women in the poorest quartile had any secondary education in 1990, only half the level of men. In contrast, 51 percent of women in the richest quartile had at least some secondary education, representing 88 percent the level of men (see table 4.3 for details).

Dollar and Gatti (1999) treat income as endogenous and include several measures of gender inequality, including:

- access and achievement in education, especially secondary education
- improvements in health, as measured by gender-disaggregated life expectancy

- indexes of legal and economic equality of women in society and marriage
- measures of women's empowerment, such as the percentage of women in parliament and the year in which women earned the right to vote.

One of the main motivations in considering a number of inequality measures is that some countries may be egalitarian in one measure but not others. Dollar and Gatti (1999, 4) note the positive correlation between gender inequality measures and per capita income of about 60 percent for all measures except women in parliament (43 percent) and secondary education attainment (28 percent). They explain gender inequality as a function of per capita income, civil liberties, economic policy, religious preference, and regional factors. Gender inequality is measured by inequality in secondary education attainment, specifically the share of the adult population for which some secondary schooling is the highest level of attainment. The data cover up to 127 countries and three five-year periods (1975–79 to 1990), yielding some 400 observations (figure 4.2).

By measuring differences in female secondary attainment and controlling for male achievement and other variables, Dollar and Gatti (1999) find a convex relationship between secondary attainment and per capita gross national product (GNP), suggesting that increases in income lead to

Figure 4.2   Attainment of at Least Secondary Education and Per Capita Income

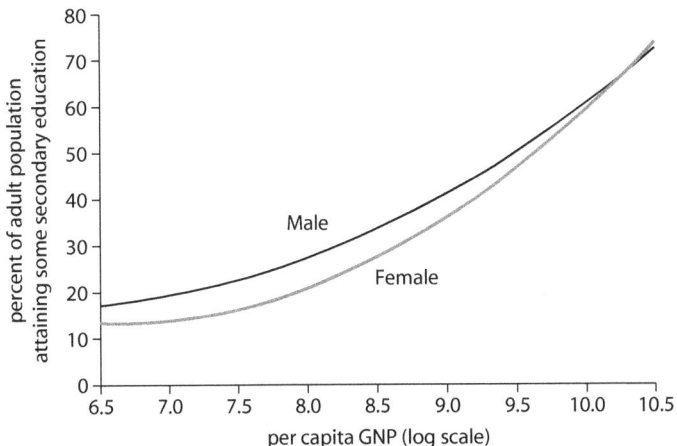

Source: Dollar and Gatti 1999, 39.

a narrowing of gender inequality in education.[6] The shape of the relationship implies that the effect is minor as countries move from very low annual income ($500 per capita) to lower-middle annual income ($2,000 per capita). It is only when countries move from lower-middle to higher income that the positive relationship between income and educational attainment for women becomes significant. The authors find that regional differences, religious preferences, and the extent of civil liberties in a society can partially explain differences in educational attainment among women (table 4.5). Controlling for the male level of secondary education, the results suggest that a high level of secondary educational attainment among women is associated with other Christian denominations and respect for civil liberties. A low level of secondary educational attainment among women is weakly associated with the Muslim and

Table 4.5   Measures of Gender Inequality (Two-Stage Least Squares Regressions)

Measure	Life expectancy	Economic equality	Equality in marriage	Women in parliament
Male Level	1.02	—	—	—
	(8.8)			
Ln (GNP per capita)	–6.61	–3.36	–0.66	–1.38
	(0.42)	(2.06)	(0.16)	(2.49)
[Ln (GNP per capita)]²	0.46	0.24	0.04	0.08
	(0.53)	(2.23)	(0.20)	(2.5)
Civil liberties	–0.05	0.01	–0.02	–0.003
	(0.31)	(0.21)	(0.26)	(0.34)
Muslim	0.006	0.001	–0.008	–0.0002
	(0.87)	(0.72)	(2.57)	(0.56)
Roman Catholic	–0.001	0.001	–0.004	–0.001
	(0.31)	(0.67)	(1.39)	(2.12)
Other Christian denominations	–0.002	–0.0005	0.008	–0.003
	(0.03)	(0.04)	(0.45)	(1.52)
Hindu	–0.02	0.002	–0.002	0.0002
	(1.43)	(0.55)	(0.41)	(0.17)
Shinto	–0.32	–0.35	–0.32	–0.05
	(1.87)	(6.89)	(6.16)	(3.5)
N	235	130	129	129
P- value for F-test on income	0.01	0.02	0.79	0.04
P- value for OIR test[a]	0.33	0.71	0.13	0.32

Source: Dollar and Gatti 1999, 31.
Note: Values in parentheses are P-values.
a. OIR = overidentifying restriction.

Hindu religions, with large positive coefficients on the Shinto variable and the indicator variable for Latin America.[7]

Regarding the other measures of gender inequality and their relationship to income growth and other cultural variables, Dollar and Gatti (1999) find:

- a convex relationship between economic equality under the law and per capita income
- a convex relationship between women in parliament and per capita income
- a significant and positive relationship between the life expectancy differential and per capita income[8]
- no significant relationship between women's rights in marriage and per capita income
- no consistent relationship between civil liberties and improvement in health, indexes of legal and economic equality of women in society and marriage, or measures of women's empowerment
- strong joint explanatory power of religious variables for improvement in health, indexes of legal and economic equality of women in society and marriage, and measures of women's empowerment.[9]

In summary, Dollar and Gatti (1999) find a causal relationship between per capita income and all measures of gender equality except marriage rights, suggesting that policies that promote growth in per capita income should lead to greater gender equality. The effect, however, is not instantaneous. The convex shape of the relationship suggests that the relationship between gender inequality, as measured by secondary educational attainment among women, and per capita income is relatively weak or nonexistent as countries move from low-income to lower-middle-income status. The relationship is stronger and positive as countries move from middle-income to higher-income status.

Volart (2004, 1) shows that discrimination in the labor market may slow economic growth and development in the short run. Volart develops a theoretical model of gender discrimination in India, hypothesizing that "gender discrimination against women in the market place reduces the available talent in an economy, which has negative economic consequences."

Empirical results from India based on Volart's model suggest that discrimination slows economic development. A 10 percent increase in the ratio of female to male managers in India would increase total output per capita by 2 percent, whereas a 10 percent increase in the ratio of female to male workers would increase total output per capita by 8 percent. The effects of gender discrimination are stronger in certain sectors of the economy, in particular sectors requiring higher skills. Lower ratios of female to male workers reduce output in both the agricultural and non-agricultural sectors, whereas lower ratios of female to male managers reduce output in nonagricultural sectors only. More worrisome are the indications in Volart's study that suggest that economic growth does not inherently reduce gender inequality. Even richer states continue to have lower ratios of female to male labor participation, suggesting the continued presence of discriminatory social norms. In such cases, targeted policies, such as those that encourage women's education and advancement in the labor market, are critical to change entrenched social norms and promote economic development.

At the other end of the spectrum are studies that indicate a positive relationship between gender inequality and income growth. Seguino (2000, 1212), for example, looks at a 21-year period (1975–95) in the history of a set of countries with a large share of exports produced in women-dominated manufacturing industries. The empirical results support two hypotheses: (a) that "gender inequality which works to lower women's wages relative to men's is a stimulus to growth in export-oriented economies" and (b) that the "growth effect of gender wage differentials is transmitted via the stimulus to investment, serving as a signal of profitability."

Since the 1980s, numerous empirical studies have examined the effects of trade and trade policies on economic growth, challenging the concept of exogenous technical progress. Although the results have been mixed, Seguino (2000, 1212) notes the importance of human capital in the growth equations, suggesting that "exports are associated with gains in output primarily for those countries with sufficient human capital to absorb new technologies." Furthermore, the economic structure of a country appears to influence the impact of trade on growth. Some studies find a positive relationship between the ratio of manufactured exports to GDP and economic growth (although this is not the case in primary commodity countries; see Levin and Raut 1997 and Sachs and Warner 1997). Seguino therefore hypothesizes that gender inequality as measured by discriminatory lower wages for women has a positive effect on technical progress and growth through the following mechanism: gender inequality leads to export expansion, which leads to investment, resulting in economic growth.

Seguino (2000, 1223) narrowly defines the causal link to investigate the "effects of discriminatorily low wages for women on: (a) exports, and therefore technological change and productivity growth, and (b) investment." The findings suggest that, across and within countries over time, there is a positive relationship between gender wage inequality and growth through both effects.[10]

Economic Growth and Gender Inequality

A number of studies examine the effect of growth on gender inequality. By aiming to explain gender inequality through economic growth or development, the studies bridge the gap between the economic growth theory approaches (neoclassical and endogenous growth theory) and the WID and GAD approaches. The study by Forsythe, Korzeniewicz, and Durrant (2000) illustrates the relevance of all three approaches to understanding the effect of economic growth on gender equality.

Forsythe, Korzeniewicz, and Durrant (2000) develop a model in which cross-national and time series data are used to investigate the effect of economic growth on the status of women and gender equality. The dependent variable—gender inequality, measured using the United Nation's GDI—is regressed on income and its quadratic and regional dummies and variables for religion. The cross-section study suggests that the Muslim variable is positively related to gender inequality, the Latin American variable is negatively related, and the level of economic development is not significant. The time series study suggests a curvilinear relationship between the level of economic development and gender inequality. Moreover, countries with the highest level of inequality are more likely to experience the greatest decline in inequality, except in predominantly Muslim countries. The results support the neoclassical and WID approaches by demonstrating a positive relationship between improvements in gender equality and economic development. Furthermore, the curvilinear relationship is consistent with the WID approach, as outlined earlier. The fact that gender inequality was significant only in the time series study lends support to the GAD approach, highlighting the complex factors that underlie a reduction in inequality.

Dollar and Gatti (1999) consider whether gender inequality affects growth. They focus on the difference between male and female secondary attainment. The growth equation derived by Dollar and Gatti (1999) is typical in its attempt to explain income growth as a function of some initial conditions, including per capita income and policies that affect the business environment; it is atypical in that it includes gender as well.[11] The final conclusion suggests that secondary education of women has an economically significant impact on growth. In fact, Dollar and Gatti (1999, 20) find that increasing the share of adult women with secondary education by 1 percentage point (in countries with higher initial education) results in an increase in per capita income growth of 0.3 percent.

Conclusion

This chapter examined the relationship between gender and economic growth on a number of levels. First, it looked at the data for a statistical relationship between gender equalities and economic growth. Many studies have focused on the correlation between measures of gender equality and economic growth. A summary of these studies suggests that gender equality measures for women's education, health, economic rights, marriage rights, and participation in parliament are all positively linked to economic growth. The contrast between women in poor and rich countries is striking, with women in poorer countries faring much worse on these indicators of gender equality.

These studies provide valuable information, but they suggest correlation, not causation. To establish causation, it is necessary to model economic growth predicated on these indicators to assess their contribution, if any, to the growth process.

The chapter reviewed the literature on models of economic growth that incorporated gender. It discussed various theoretical approaches, including the modernization-neoclassical approach, WID, the critical feminism and development approach, GAD, and the endogenous growth theory.

The chapter then examined the empirical studies of gender inequalities and economic growth, noting that the reciprocal relationship between the two makes it difficult to fully isolate the effect of each factor. The empirical literature falls into three categories: studies that find a positive relationship between gender equality and economic growth, studies that find a positive relationship between gender inequality and economic growth, and studies that identify facets of gender discrimination that slow economic growth.

The chapter concluded with a brief overview of the studies that examine the effect of economic growth on gender inequality. This approach brings together the conclusions from the theoretical approaches considered earlier in the chapter. It bridges the gap between the economic approaches of neoclassical/modernization and endogenous growth theory with those from the WID and GAD approaches.

Notes

1. Udry (1996) and Saito (1994) note that equalizing female access to agricultural inputs in Burkina Faso, Kenya, and Zambia resulted in a 10–20 percent increase in output.

2. Gender discrimination in the labor market in developed countries is usually identified in differential wage rates between men and women; in developing countries, discrimination takes the form of differential access to wage employment (Collier 1994).

3. A number of empirical studies have identified a curvilinear relationship between gender inequalities and economic growth (see Dollar and Gatti 1999). Pampel and Tanaka (1986) find such a relationship between patterns of female labor force participation and economic development for data from 1965 and 1970. See also Evenson (1983) and Chafetz (1984).

4. Romer (1986) challenged the law of diminishing returns upon which the neoclassical growth theory rests. He developed endogenous growth theory, which relies on constant returns (to a factor). He finds no automatic relationship between how poor an economy is and how rich it can grow. As a result, contrary to the teachings of the neoclassical model, income disparities can continue.

5. Lucas (1988) first introduced human capital into endogenous growth theory.

6. Various specifications of the model are estimated using different estimation techniques, including ordinary least squares, two-stage least squares, and fixed effects. Varying the estimation techniques provides greater confidence in the results—that is, the relationship between gender inequality, as measured by secondary attainment, and income is causal. The convex relationship holds in both the two-stage least squares regression (using rule of law and black market premium for per capita income and per capita income squared) and the fixed-effects regression, although the fixed-effects relationship is weaker than the least squares regression. The authors also consider different specifications for the education differentials: female secondary attainment and secondary differential (female attainment minus male attainment) and female postsecondary attainment (the proportion of the female population with at least some secondary plus higher attainment) and differential (female postsecondary attainment minus male postsecondary attainment). There is no relationship between variables at low levels, but as the levels increase, so does the relationship (see figure 4.2).

7. The underlying data reveal that Latin America has relatively low attainment in education compared with East Asia or Europe and Central Asia but lower gender inequality as well. South Asia has the largest gender differential.

8. This result is based on the F-test. It is difficult to make inferences on the shape of the curve.

9. Dollar and Gatti (1999) caution against making inferences based solely on one indicator of inequality. For example, they note a strong positive relationship between the Shinto variable and female secondary attainment. This observation could lead to the conclusion that Shinto women have high status in Japan. In fact, the Shinto variable exhibits a strongly negative relationship with all of the other measures of gender inequality (see table 4.5).

10. "The key seems to lie in the socialization of women who are less inclined than men, at least in the sample of countries used in this study, to protest income inequality sufficiently to slow investment and growth" (Seguino 2000, 1227).

11. Dollar and Gatti (1999, 10) refer to "a large literature estimating variants of this (the growth equation) without reference to gender, beginning with Barro (1991)."

Bibliography

Agarwal, B. 1974. "Women and Technological Change in Agriculture: The Asian and African Experience." In *Technology and Rural Women*, ed. I. Ahmed. London: Allen and Unwin.

Afshar, H., and C. Dennis, eds. 1992. *Women and Adjustment Policies in the Third World*. London: Macmillan.

Bandarage, A. 1984. "Women in Development: Liberalism, Marxism and Marxist-Feminism." *Development and Change* 15 (4): 495–515.

Barro, R. 1991. "Economic Growth in a Cross-Section of Countries." *Quarterly Journal of Economics* 106 (May): 407–43.

Barro, R., and J.-W. Lee. 1994. "Sources of Economic Growth." *Carnegie-Rochester Conference Series on Public Policy* 40: 1–46.

Benería, L. 1982. "Introduction." In *Women and Development. The Sexual Division of Labor in Rural Societies*, ed. L. Benería. New York: Praeger.

Boserup, E. 1970. *Women's Role in Economic Development*. New York: St. Martin's Press.

Buchman, C. 1996. "The Debt Crisis, Structural Adjustment and Women's Education: Implications for Status and Social Development." *International Journal of Comparative Sociology* 37: 5–30.

Chafetz, J. S. 1984. *Sex and Advantage: A Comparative Macro-Structural Theory of Sex Stratification*. Totowa, NJ: Rowman & Allanheld.

Collier, P. 1994. "Gender Aspects of Labor Allocation during Structural Adjustment: Theoretical Framework and the Africa Experience." In *Labor Markets in an Era of Adjustment*, ed. S. Horton, R. Hanbur, and D. Mazumbur. Washington, DC: World Bank.

Dollar, D., and R. Gatti. 1999. "Gender Inequality, Income, and Growth: Are Good Times Good for Women?" Working Paper Series 1, World Bank, Development Research Group, Poverty Reduction and Economic Management, Washington, DC.

Draper, E. 1985. "Women's Work and Development in Latin America." *Studies in Comparative International Development* 20 (1): 3–30.

Elson, D. 1995. "Male Bias in the Development Process: An Overview." In *Male Bias in the Development Process*, ed. Diane Elson. Manchester, U.K.: Manchester University Press.

Emeagwali, G. T. 1995. *Women Pay the Price. Structural Adjustment in Africa and the Caribbean.* Trenton, NJ: Africa World Press.

Evenson, R. 1983. "The Allocation of Women's Time: An International Comparison." *Behavioral Science Research* 17 (3–4): 196–215.

Folbre, N. 1986. "Cleaning House: New Perspectives on Households and Economic Development." *Journal of Development Economics* 22 (1): 5–40.

Forsythe, N., R. P. Korzeniewicz, and V. Durrant. 2000. "Gender Inequalities and Economic Growth: A Longitudinal Evaluation." *Culture and Change* 48 (April): 573–617.

Galor, O., and D. N. Weil. 1996. "The Gender Gap, Fertility and Growth." *American Economic Review* 86 (3): 374–87.

Humana, C. 1992. *World Human Rights Guide.* New York: Oxford University Press.

Jütting, J. P., C. Morrisson, J. Dayton-Johnson, and D. Drechsler. 2006. "Measuring Gender (In)Equality: Introducing the Gender, Institutions and Development Database (GID)." Working Paper No. 247, OECD Development Centre, Organisation for Economic Co-operation and Development, Paris.

Kabeer, N. 1994. *Reversed Realities: Gender Hierarchies in Development Thought.* London: Verso.

Killick, T. 1995. "Structural Adjustment and Poverty Alleviation: An Interpretative Survey." *Development and Change* 26 (April): 305–31.

Klasen, S. 1998. *Gender Inequality and Growth in Sub-Saharan Africa: Some Preliminary Findings.* Department of Economics, University of Munich.

Kuznets, S. 1955. "Economic Growth and Income Inequality." *American Economic Review* 45 (1): 1–28.

Lagerlof, N-P. 2003. "Gender Equality and Long-Run Growth." *Journal of Economic Growth* 8 (4): 403–26.

Lantican, C. P., C. H. Gladwin, and J. L. Seale Jr. 1996. "Income and Gender Inequalities in Asia: Testing Alternative Theories of Development." *Economic Development and Cultural Change* 44 (January): 235–63.

Lele, U. 1986. "Women and Structural Transformation." *Economic Development and Cultural Change* 34 (2): 195–221.

Levin, A., and L. Raut. 1997. "Complementarities between Exports and Human Capital in Economic Growth: Evidence from Semi-Industrialized Countries." *Economic Development and Cultural Change* 46 (1): 155–74.

Lucas, R. E. 1988. "On the Mechanics of Economic Development." *Journal of Monetary Economics* 21: 3–42.

Marchand, M. H., and J. L. Parpart, eds. 1995. *Feminism, Postmodernism, Development.* London: Routledge.

Moore, G., and G. Shackman. 1996. "Gender and Authority: A Cross-National Study." *Social Science Quarterly* 77 (June): 273–88.

Moser, C. O. N. 1993. *Gender Planning and Development Theory, Practice, and Training.* London: Routledge.

Nuss, S., and L. Majka. 1983. "The Economic Integration of Women: A Cross-National Investigation." *Work and Occupations* 10: 29–48.

Pampel, F. C., and K. Tanaka. 1986. "Economic Development and Female Labor Force Participation: A Reconsideration." *Social Forces* 64 (3): 599–619.

Parpart, J. L. 1993. "Who Is the Other? A Postmodern Feminist Critique of Women and Development Theory and Practice." *Development and Change* 24 (3): 439–64.

Ramirez, R. O., Y. Soysal, and S. Shanahan. 1997. "The Changing Logic of Political Citizenship: Cross-National Acquisition of Women's Suffrage Rights, 1890 to 1990." *American Sociological Review* 62 (October): 735–45.

Romer, P. 1986. "Increasing Returns and Long-Run Growth." *Journal of Political Economy* 94: 1002–38.

Sachs, J., and A. Warner. 1997. "Economic Reform and the Process of Global Integration." *Brookings Papers on Economic Activity* 1: 1–118.

Saito, K. A., with contribution from H. Mekonnen and D. Spurling. 1994. "Raising the Productivity of Women Farmers in Sub-Saharan Africa." World Bank Discussion Paper, Africa Technical Department Series 230, Washington, DC.

Seguino, S. 2000. "Gender Inequality and Economic Growth: A Cross-Country Analysis." *World Development* 28 (7): 1211–30.

Semyonov, M. 1980. "The Social Context of Women's Labor Force Participation: A Comparative Analysis." *American Journal of Sociology* 86 (November): 534–50.

Sparr, P. 1994. "Feminist Critiques of Structural Adjustment." In *Mortgaging Women's Lives: Feminist Critiques of Structural Adjustment,* ed. P. Sparr. London: Zed Books.

Staundt, K. 1985. *Women, Foreign Assistance and Advocacy Administration.* New York: Praeger.

Stotsky, J. 2006. "Gender and Its Relevance to Macroeconomic Policy: A Survey." IMF Working Paper WP/06/233, International Monetary Fund, Washington, DC.

Tinker, I. 1976. "The Adverse Impact of Development on Women." In *Women and World Development*, ed. I. Tinker and M. B. Bramsen. Washington, DC: Overseas Development Council.

Udry, C. 1996. "Gender, Agricultural Production and the Theory of the Household." *Journal of Political Economy* 104 (5): 1010–46.

Volart, B. E. 2004. *Gender Discrimination and Growth: Theory and Evidence from India*. DEDPS 42, STICERD (Suntory and Toyota International Centres for Economics and Related Disciplines), London School of Economics.

Walters, B. 1995. "Engendering Macroeconomics: A Reconsideration of Growth Theory." *World Development* 23 (11): 1869–80.

Ward, K. 1984. *Women in the World System: Its Impact on Status and Fertility.* New York: Praeger.

Youssef, N. H. 1972. "Differential Labor Force Participation of Women in Latin America and Middle Eastern Countries: The Influence of Family Characteristics." *Social Forces* 51: 135–53.

CHAPTER 5

Gender and the Labor Market

Gender inequality manifests itself most obviously in labor markets. Women face greater barriers than men to finding decent and productive work. Women's labor force participation has risen in some but not all regions. Moreover, the quality of work and working conditions have not always kept pace with increases in participation. Persistent gender inequalities in wages suggest that the labor market is not operating freely.

Women continue to be overrepresented in unpaid and informal work. The agricultural and service sectors employ more women than men, yet they often pay women less for similar work. These inequalities are especially significant in developing economies, where women are more likely to be among the working poor—those who work but do not earn enough to lift themselves above the $1 a day poverty line. Indeed, women make up at least 60 percent of the world's working poor (ILO 2004).

The gender division of labor also remains sharp in industrial and urban societies. Worldwide most jobs are dominated by one gender or the other. For example, women make up 41 percent of the nonagricultural labor force in the Organisation for Economic Co-operation and Development (OECD) countries but are disproportionately shunted into service jobs: women constitute 62 percent of service workers, compared with only 15 percent of production workers (Anker 1998, 171).

For specific professions, such as nursing, the proportion of female employees can be as high as 82 percent (Anker 1998, 264). Although there is an undeniable concentration of women in low-paid occupations and sectors, the degree of job segregation by sex makes a comparison between men's and women's work difficult. These disparities also make it difficult for policy makers and workers to determine equal pay and working conditions.

The following sections present data that highlight gender inequalities in the labor market and show the progress that has been made in some areas and regions. The discussion extends beyond the data to include a commentary on how gender inequality in labor markets affects macro-economic policy. The chapter also highlights the vulnerability of women in the world of work and includes a discussion of the third Millennium Development Goal (MDG 3), which focuses on redressing gender dispar-ities and empowering women.

Gender Inequality and the Labor Market

Specialization of work is one reason why gender inequality exists in the labor market. Tradition and customs often dictate the types of work that men and women can perform. The social context is paramount in influencing who may do what, thereby affecting overall output. Tibaijuka (1994) shows that improving gender equality in the produc-tion of bananas and coffee for export in the Kagera Region in Tanzania would increase a village's income by 10 percent, with the productivity of labor rising 15 percent and the productivity of capital rising 44 per-cent. Collier (1994, 285) shows that gender inequality in the labor market constrained tea cultivation in Kenya in areas with female-headed households, as they were less likely than male-headed house-holds to grow tea, despite the fact that women do most of the work on tea plantations and households with more women are more likely to grow tea.

Collier (1994) considers possible reasons why gender inequalities arise in the labor market (in Africa) by focusing on four processes that lead women to face constraints on their economic activity that are dif-ferent from those facing men. First, women may encounter discrimina-tion outside the household.[1] Discrimination in many developing economies takes the form of differential access to formal paid employ-ment. For example, in rural Tanzania, men with secondary education had a 75 percent chance of obtaining formal employment, compared with a 50 percent chance for equally educated women (Collier 1994, citing Collier, Radwan, and Wangwe 1986).

Second, there is a tendency among both men and women to copy role models of the same sex. Thus if a new economic opportunity arises and initially taken up by men, men will continue to take it up, with women remaining on the sidelines.

Third, asymmetric rights between men and women within the house-hold become entrenched over time. One example is in rural Africa, where women bear responsibilities for child rearing, growing food for subsistence, gathering fuel and water, and cooking while men are responsible for meeting the household's cash needs and allocating land. Another example, from the Kyrgyz Republic, suggests that 24.8 percent of women were hindered from working outside the home (compared with just 1.5 percent of men) because of housekeeping duties and taking care of children, sick people, or the elderly (Morrison and Lamana 2006).

Fourth, women bear the burden of reproduction and child rearing. During this time, skills may decline and long-term contracts, common in the labor market, may be terminated (Collier 1994, 287). These four processes tend to shunt women into certain sectors of the labor market and make it difficult for them to move across sectors.

According to the International Labour Organization (2007), the segregation of occupations by sex is changing, albeit slowly; additional investment in women's education and training is needed to keep change moving forward. Between 1996 and 2006, the share of women in wage and salaried work increased from 42.9 to 47.9 percent (ILO 2007). Still, fewer women than men have paid work, especially in the world's poorer regions. Interestingly, time-use studies suggest that women work more total hours than men (Stotsky 2006).

Even when women migrate, they tend to be overrepresented in stereo-typical woman's occupations. The United Nations Population Fund (UNFPA 2006) estimates that there are 95 million female migrants, who account for half of all migrants and contribute hugely to remittances. Migration for women takes place across all age and income groups. Women migrants often face significant challenges in their host country, especially if discrimination because of race, class, or religion is a factor. Many women migrate illegally and are unaware of their rights. Figure 5.1 shows the trends in female migration for three sample years between 1995 and 2005.

Figure 5.1   Female Share of International Migrants, 1995, 2000, and 2005

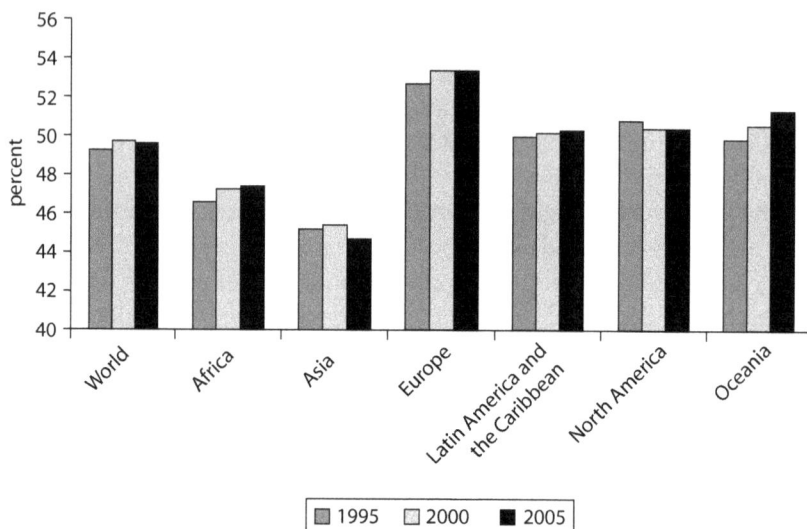

Source: ILO 2007, 9.

Labor Force Participation Rates

The labor force participation rate (LFPR) is the share of the working-age population that is either employed or unemployed and looking for a job. The female LFPR, which indicates how many women of working age are active in the labor market, has been increasing in recent years, a sign that more women are seeking to achieve economic independence (ILO 2004).

Table 5.1 shows the change in the LFPR for men and women over a 10-year period. The total female labor force worldwide was 1.2 billion in 2006, up from 1.1 billion a decade earlier. Over the 10-year period, the female LFPR declined to 52.4 in 2006, from 53 percent in 1996. The ILO attributes this decline to the increasing numbers of young women receiving education and the increasing share of older women in the labor force. More recent data indicate that the LFPR in 2008 was 52.6 percent for women and 77.5 percent for men (ILO 2009). Although the gap is narrowing, it still stands at 25 percentage points. Women made up 40.5 percent of the global labor force in 2008, up from 39.9 percent a decade earlier (ILO 2009).

Figure 5.2 breaks down the LFPR data by sex and region. It shows that the female LFPR increased and the gap between male and female LFPRs

Table 5.1   Global Labor Market Indicators, 1996 and 2006

	Women		Men		Total	
Indicator	1996	2006	1996	2006	1996	2006
Labor force (millions)	1,052.0	1,238.9	1,592.2	1,852.0	2,644.2	3,090.9
Employment (millions)	985.4	1,157.1	1,497.5	1,738.6	2,482.8	2,895.7
Unemployment (millions)	66.7	81.8	94.7	113.4	161.4	195.2
Labor force participation rate (percent)	53.0	52.4	80.5	78.8	66.7	65.5
Employment-to-population ratio (percent)	49.6	48.9	75.7	74.0	62.6	61.4
Unemployment rate (percent)	6.3	6.6	5.9	6.1	6.1	6.3

Source: ILO 2007, 14.

Figure 5.2   Male and Female Labor Force Participation Rates, by Region, 1996 and 2006

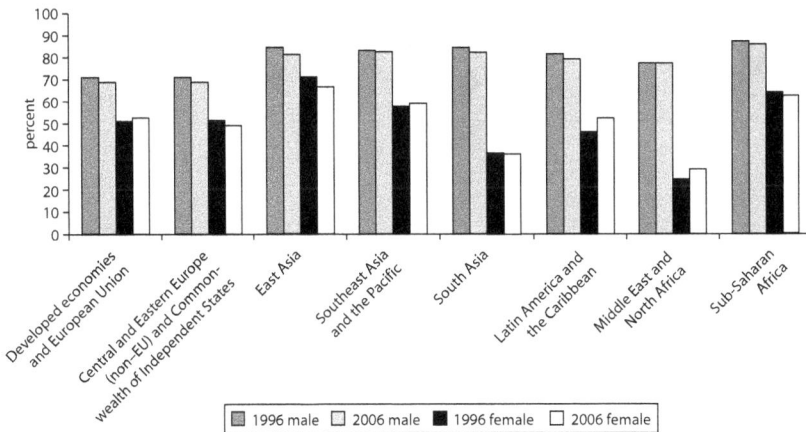

Source: ILO 2007, 3.

decreased over the 10-year period from 1996 to 2006 in four regions: developed economies and the European Union (EU), Southeast Asia and the Pacific, Latin America and the Caribbean, and the Middle East and North Africa. During the same period, the male LFPR declined in all regions except the Middle East and North Africa, where it remained the same. The female LFPR in the remaining regions fared less well over the 10-year period—in fact, between 1996 and 2006, the gap between the male and female LFPRs grew by 0.3 percent in Sub-Saharan Africa and by 1.0 percent in East Asia.

Table 5.2 shows the regional LFPRs for men and women for 2007 and 2009. Globally, the LFPR is estimated to have remained the same for women and declined marginally for men. Across regions, the estimated increase in the LFPR for women is highest in Sub-Saharan Africa, the Middle East and North Africa, and Latin America and the Caribbean (a 0.6–0.7 percentage point increase). The increase for the other regions is marginal (0.1 percentage point), with a decrease projected in East Asia (0.3 percentage points). For men, LFPRs fell, except in Southeast Asia and the Pacific, the Middle East and North Africa, and Sub-Saharan Africa, which all showed marginal projected increases of at least 0.1 percentage point.

Despite improvement in several regions, the gap between the male and female LFPRs remains wide. The gender gap—the number of economically active women per 100 men—indicates the magnitude of gender inequality. Just 67 women per 100 men were active globally in 2006, and

Table 5.2   Labor Force Participation Rates for Women and Men, by Region, 2007 and 2009

(percent)

Region	Women 2007	2009	Men 2007	2009	Total 2007	2009
World	51.6	51.6	77.8	77.7	64.7	64.7
Developed economies	52.8	52.9	69.1	68.6	60.7	60.5
Central and Southeastern Europe (non–EU) and Commonwealth of Independent States	50.5	50.6	69.2	69.0	59.3	59.2
East Asia	66.8	66.5	79.6	79.4	73.4	73.1
Southeast Asia and the Pacific	57.2	57.4	81.9	82.0	69.4	69.5
South Asia	34.8	34.9	81.7	81.6	58.9	58.8
Latin America and the Caribbean	51.0	51.7	80.1	79.7	65.2	65.4
Middle East	24.8	25.4	75.1	75.3	51.2	51.5
North Africa	27.3	27.4	75.5	76.4	51.3	51.8
Sub-Saharan Africa	61.9	62.6	81.1	81.2	71.4	71.7

Source: ILO 2010, 50.
Note: Figures for 2009 are preliminary estimates.

the figures vary widely by region. Eighty-one women per 100 men were active in developed and transition economies in 2006, and the gender gap in East Asia was 79. In contrast, just 37 women per 100 men were active in the Middle East and North Africa in 2006, and only 42 women per 100 men were active in South Asia (table 5.3).

As the ILO (2007, 3) notes, "taken on their own, rising or high labor force participation rates do not necessarily mean that labor markets are developing positively for women." Is gender equality in the labor market improving? Are wage gaps and discrimination reducing LFPRs? Are women finding the type of work they want? Does the fact that more women are in school account for the lower female LFPR? What are the characteristics of women's work compared with men's work? The following sections shed some light on these questions.

Education

According to the ILO (2007, 2), "there is considerable doubt that women get the same chances as men to develop their skills throughout their working lives." Why? Cultural factors such as religion and gender discrimination play a part. Women are also often segregated into low-paying occupations, which may discourage investment in girls' education (World Bank 2007).

Although female education levels have improved, low-income countries still face significant challenges if they are to achieve MDG 3. More young women are literate than was the case 15 years ago, yet women still account for two-thirds of the almost 800 million adults who cannot read or write (ILO 2007). Figure 5.3 examines the literacy

Table 5.3   Gender Gap in Employment, 2006

Region	Number of economically active women per 100 men
World	66.9
Developed economies	81.4
Transition economies	81.0
East Asia	79.3
Southeast Asia	72.7
South Asia	41.8
Latin America and the Caribbean	69.5
Middle East and North Africa	36.7
Sub-Saharan Africa	74.8

Source: ILO 2007, 14.

Figure 5.3   Literacy Rates among Youth (15–24 Years), by Region, 1990 and 2005

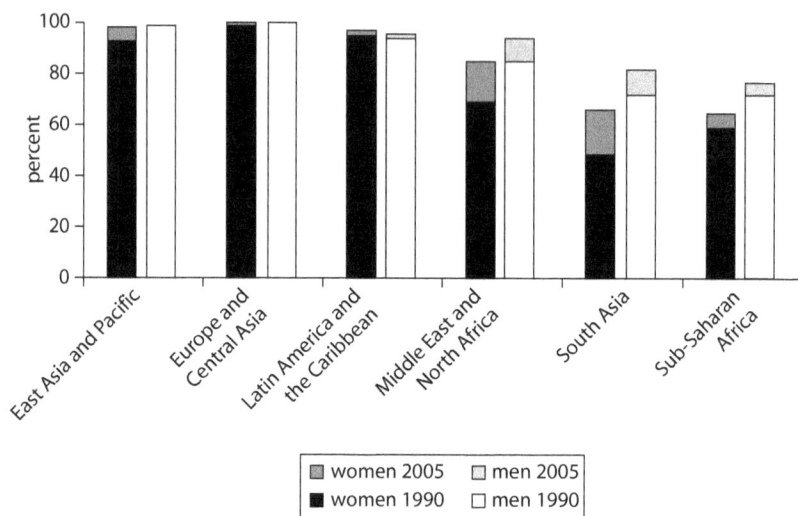

Source: World Bank 2008, 255.

rate—defined as a person's ability to read and write—by region between 1990 and 2005. It shows that women have the lowest literacy rates in South Asia and the Middle East and North Africa. Significant progress is noted across all regions, and literacy rates have increased, especially in regions starting from lower levels (World Bank 2008).

Among the indicators used to assess the progress toward MDG 3 are the ratio of girls' to boys' enrollment in primary, secondary, and tertiary education and the ratio of literate women to men 15–24. Figure 5.4 illustrates the progress in girls' enrollment rates for primary, secondary, and tertiary education between 1990 and 2005.

Most low-income countries achieved gender parity in ratios of primary school enrollment and literacy between 1995 and 2005 (Lewis and Lockheed 2006; World Bank 2007). Eighty-three of the 106 countries for which data are available achieved parity in both primary and secondary school enrollment rates (table 5.4).

Several challenges remain to achieving MDG 3. As shown in table 5.4, 22 states and countries, 16 of which are in Sub-Saharan Africa, are unlikely to meet the target by 2015. Sixty percent of school dropouts are girls (ILO 2007). And women in excluded groups—that is, in populations that are socially excluded based on income, location, race, ethnicity, or

Figure 5.4   Progress in Girls' Enrollment Rates, by Region, 1990–2005

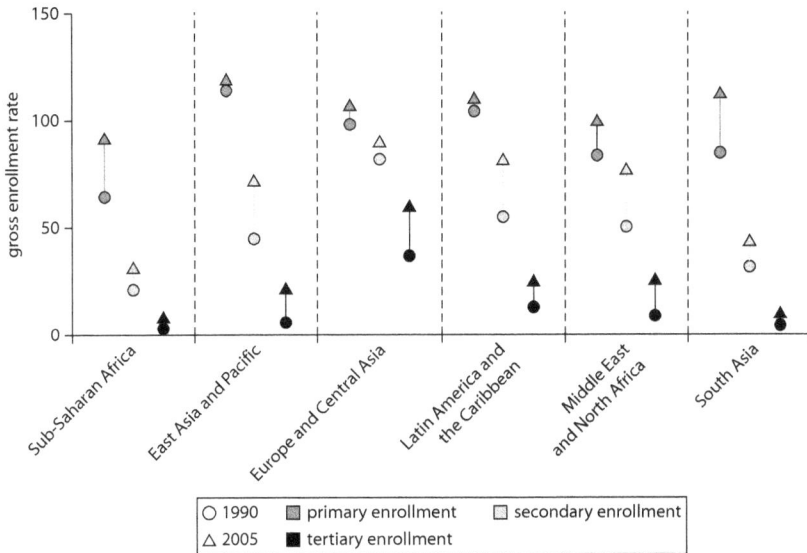

Source: World Bank 2007, 112.

Table 5.4   Attainment of Gender Parity in Primary and Secondary Education Enrollment, by Region, 2005 and 2015
(number of countries)

Region	Achieved target by 2005	On track to achieve target by 2015	Off track or unlikely to achieve target by 2015	No data	Total
Sub-Saharan Africa	10	1	16	21	48
East Asia and Pacific	13	0	0	11	24
Europe and Central Asia	22	0	1	4	27
Latin America and the Caribbean	27	0	0	4	31
Middle East and North Africa	8	0	3	3	14
South Asia	3	0	2	3	8
Total	83	1	22	46	152
of which: Fragile states	5	0	9	21	35

Source: World Bank 2007, 114.
Note: The "No data" column indicates the number of countries with missing data at the start of the period, at the end of the period, or both.

disability—in low-income countries, particularly rural areas, often face discrimination in education. Policies need to target these groups to increase their school enrollment rates.

Unemployment Rates

Figure 5.5 examines world and regional unemployment rates by sex for 2006. Globally, women were more likely to be unemployed than men (6.6 percent versus 6.1 percent). The 2006 women's unemployment rate was up from 6.3 percent in 1996. According to the ILO (2007), 81.8 million women without jobs were willing to work and actively looking for work in 2006, up 22.7 percent from 10 years earlier. These figures do not tell the whole story, however; it is important also to consider discouraged workers, who are not included in official unemployment statistics: "Given that women face higher unemployment rates, have far fewer opportunities in labor markets than men and often face social barriers to enter labor markets, it is very likely that discouragement among women is higher than among men in most countries in the developing world" (ILO 2007, 5).[2] The impact of the global financial crisis in 2008 was about equally detrimental for men and women, with the unemployment

Figure 5.5   World and Regional Overall Unemployment Rate, by Sex, 2006

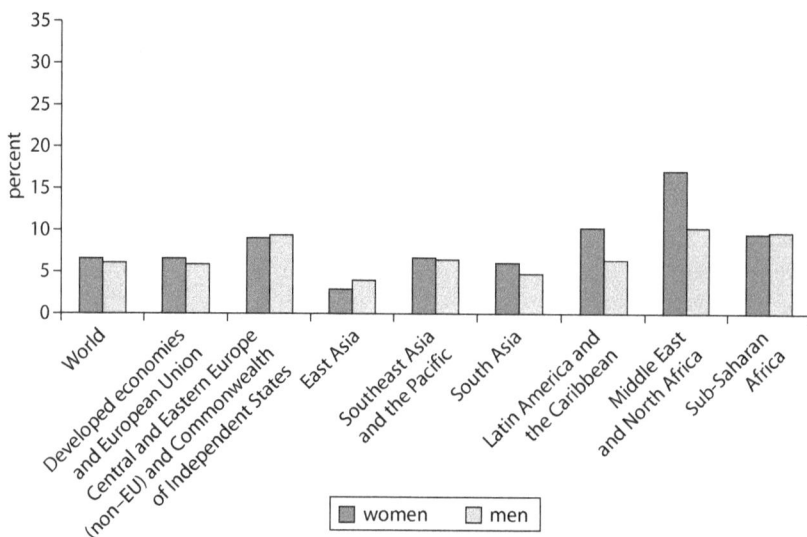

rate for women increasing by 0.8 percentage points between 2008 and 2009 and for men increasing by 0.7 percentage points.

Table 5.5 examines regional unemployment rates by sex for 2008 and 2009. Between these years, women are estimated to have experienced higher unemployment rates than men in Latin America and North Africa and broadly comparable unemployment rates as men in East Asia, Southeast Asia and the Pacific, South Asia, and Sub-Saharan Africa, suggesting little to zero impact from the financial crisis. Table 5.5 also illustrates the gender disparity in unemployment rates in the Middle East and North Africa, where the gaps are more than twice those of other regions (ILO 2010, 15).

Gender disparity exists in youth unemployment. Roughly 35.6 million women in the 15–24 age bracket were seeking employment in 2006. Figure 5.6 shows that unemployment rates for young women are far higher than those for young men in five of the regions considered: Central and Eastern Europe (non–EU) and the Commonwealth of Independent

Table 5.5   Unemployment Rate among Women and Men, by Region, 2008 and 2009

(percent)

Region	Women 2008	Women 2009	Men 2008	Men 2009	Total 2008	Total 2009
World	6.1	7.0	5.6	6.3	5.8	6.6
Developed economies	6.1	8.6	6.0	8.2	6.0	8.4
Central and South-eastern Europe (non–EU) and Commonwealth of Independent States	8.1	9.8	8.3	10.6	8.3	10.3
East Asia	3.6	3.7	4.9	5.0	4.3	4.4
Southeast Asia and the Pacific	5.5	5.9	5.2	5.5	5.3	5.6
South Asia	5.6	5.9	4.5	4.8	4.8	5.1
Latin America and the Caribbean	8.8	10.1	5.8	6.9	7.0	8.2
Middle East	14.7	15.0	7.5	7.7	9.2	9.4
North Africa	14.8	15.6	8.2	8.6	10.0	10.5
Sub-Saharan Africa	8.5	8.8	7.6	7.8	8.0	8.2

Source: ILO 2010, 46.
Note: Figures for 2009 are preliminary estimates.

Figure 5.6   World and Regional Youth Unemployment Rate, by Sex, 2006

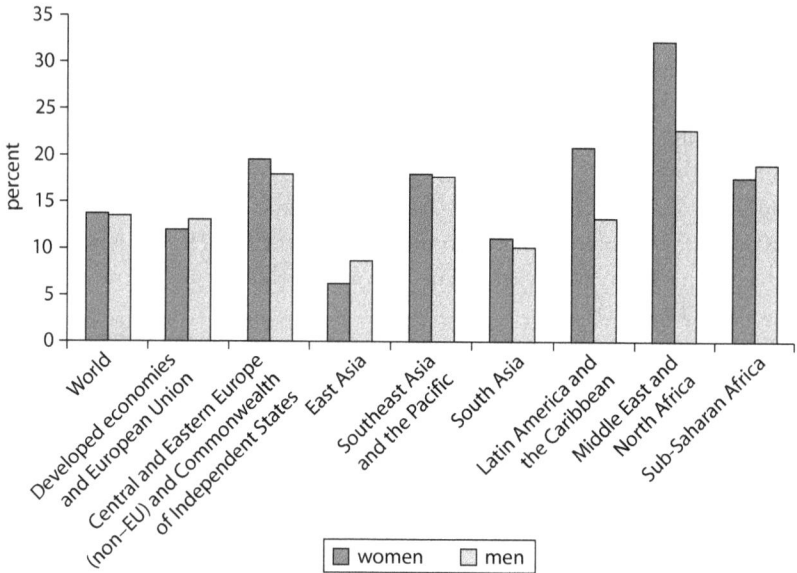

Source: ILO 2007, 4.

States (CIS), Southeast Asia and the Pacific, South Asia, Latin America and the Caribbean, and the Middle East and North Africa.

An examination of employment to population ratios (see table 5.4) suggests that in all regions, women's productive potential is not being used to the same extent as that of men. Only half of working-age women (15 and older) work, compared with more than 7 out of 10 men. The lowest employment to population ratio for women occurs in the Middle East and North Africa, followed by South Asia. In the decade between 1996 and 2006, the employment to population ratio for women worsened for the world as a whole, with Central and Eastern Europe (non–EU) and the CIS, East Asia, South Asia, and Sub-Saharan Africa leading the downward trend, with drops of more than 1 percent. The impact of the recent global crisis is seen in the decline in employment to population ratios for women (and men) in 2009 with respect to 2006. But the employment to population ratio for women increased for many regions from 2006 to 2009 (table 5.6), in particular in Southeast Asia and the Pacific and Sub-Saharan Africa. By contrast, male employment to population ratios declined in 2009 from 2006 across all regions except the Middle East and North Africa and Sub-Saharan Africa, where they remained the same.

Table 5.6   Employment to Population Ratios for Women and Men, by Region, 1996, 2006, and 2009

Region	Women			Men		
	1996	2006	2009	1996	2006	2009
World	49.6	48.3	48.0	75.7	73.5	72.8
Developed economies	46.6	49.2	48.3	65.8	64.9	63.0
Central South-eastern Europe (non–EU) and Commonwealth of Independent States	46.4	45.7	45.6	64.2	62.4	61.7
East Asia	68.8	64.8	64.0	81.1	76.4	75.4
Southeast Asia and the Pacific	55.3	53.2	54.0	80.0	77.6	77.5
South Asia	34.9	32.5	32.8	80.6	78.1	77.7
Latin America and the Caribbean	41.5	46.0	46.5	76.2	75.5	74.3
Middle East	20.4[a]	21.0	21.6	68.3[a]	69.3	69.5
North Africa		22.8	23.1		69.3	69.9
Sub-Saharan Africa	58.7	56.5	57.1	79.2	74.8	74.8

Source: ILO 2010, 50.
Note: Rates for 2009 are preliminary estimates. Rates for 1996 are from ILO 2007, 14.
a. Rates represent a combined regional total for the Middle East and North Africa.

Wage Rates

Although data across countries and regions are limited, it is clear that wage gaps between women and men persist, even in occupations dominated by women. One study of six occupational groups estimates that in most economies, women earn 90 percent or less of what their male counterparts earn (ILO 2007). Wage inequality is found across all occupations, predominantly in low-skilled occupations but also in highly skilled ones. Corley, Perardel, and Popova (2005), quoted in ILO (2007), note that the average female wage is only 88 percent of the average male wage in occupations such as accounting and computer programming. Oostendorp (2004) shows that in developing countries, globalization has led to an improvement in wages in low-skilled occupations, in which women are more highly represented, but a widening gender gap in wages among high-skilled occupations, in which men are more highly represented.

Figure 5.7 examines wage data for six occupational groups in industrial economies, Central and Eastern Europe and the CIS, and developing economies. Male and female hotel receptionists in Central and

Figure 5.7   Average Women's Earnings as a Percentage of Men's Earnings in Selected Occupations, Latest Available Year

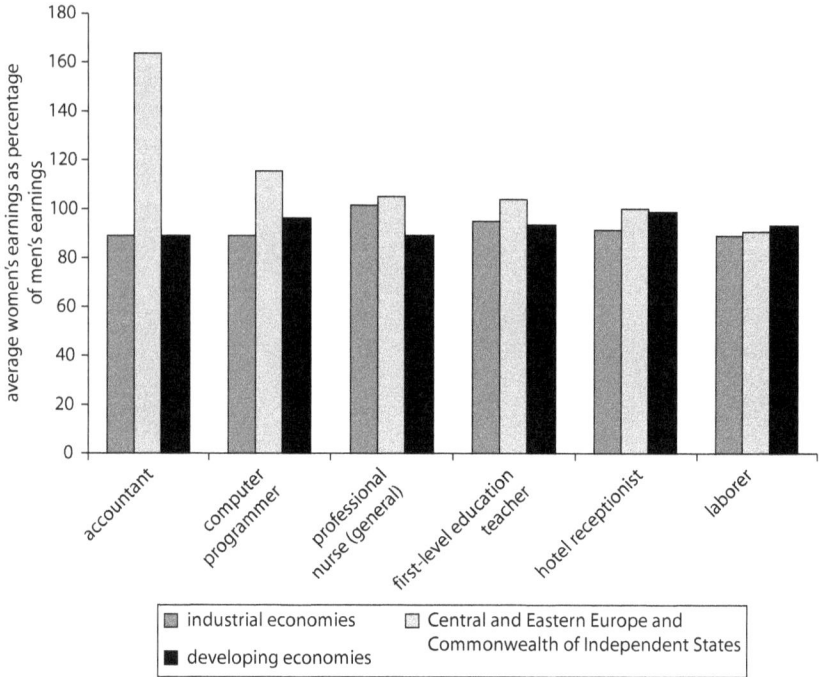

Source: ILO 2007, 12 citing ILO 2005, tables 16a and 16b.
Note: Average in this figure denotes a simple average of countries for which data were available.

Eastern Europe, the CIS, and developing economies enjoy wage parity, and female nursing professionals in industrial economies, Central and Eastern Europe, and the CIS earn slightly more than their male counterparts. Wage rates are significantly higher for female first-level teachers, computer programmers, and accountants in Central and Eastern Europe and the CIS than for men in the same professions; this gap reflects the historically greater wage equality in the planned economies of Central and Eastern Europe and the CIS, which may narrow or disappear once the few women who have successfully managed the transition process retire (ILO 2007). In all other professions and regions compared, women earn less than men.

The relationship between gender gaps and wage gaps depends on the country and the sector of employment. For example, the World Bank (2007) finds that in the countries of Sub-Saharan Africa, female LFPRs for people ages 20–49 were high, whereas the gender gap was low and women were concentrated in low-paying agricultural employment or self-employment in the nonagricultural sector.[3] Furthermore, in those countries—mainly in Europe, Central Asia, and East Asia and the Pacific—where women's participation is high, the gender gap is low, educational attainment is high for both sexes, and women earn lower wages than men in nonagricultural employment. But just 20 percent of the gender gap in wages was explained by male-female differences in observed worker or job characteristics in Poland and the Russian Federation and during the mid-1990s. The remaining gap was unexplained but considered a measure of labor market discrimination against women (World Bank 2007, 129). Persistent gender inequalities in wages indicate that the labor market is not operating freely. Differences between men's and women's outside obligations—and, by extension, bargaining power—may help explain this ongoing problem. For example, the reservation wage—the lowest wage a worker will accept for a particular job—is often lower for women than it is for men. This may reflect the fact that women's family obligations decline with their mobility; unable to move for a better-paying job, they end up accepting lower wages close to home. As noted above, in developing economies, for example, women receive lower pay than men for the same agricultural work.

Persistent wage gaps and discrimination against women in the labor market may lead to fewer women participating in the labor force. As the World Bank (2007) notes, the wage loss caused by discrimination may cause parents to invest less in their daughters' education than in their sons'.[4]

Employment by Sector

At the global level, male and female shares of employment by sector follow a regular pattern, with women employed predominantly in agriculture and services (figure 5.8). Out of the total number of employed women in 2006, 40.4 percent worked in agriculture and 42.4 percent in services. Of all working men, 37.5 percent worked in agriculture and 38.4 percent in services. This pattern was unchanged in 2008, with 35.4 percent of women employed in agriculture compared with 32.2 percent of men. The rates for service employment were 46.3 percent of women and 41.2 percent of men (ILO 2009). Meanwhile, 17.2 percent of all women worked in industry in 2006, a proportion that increased marginally to 18.3 percent in 2008.

Figure 5.8   Sectoral Employment Shares for Men and Women as a Percentage of Total Employment, 1996–2006

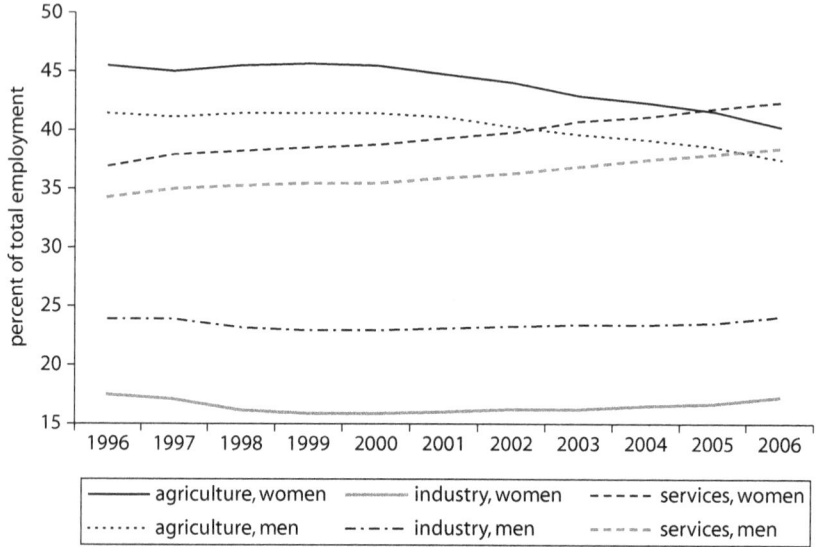

Source: ILO 2007, 7.

Table 5.7 suggests that in regions other than the non–EU European and CIS countries and Latin America and the Caribbean, women have a higher share of agricultural employment than men. Furthermore, women's agricultural employment in the Middle East and North Africa actually increased from 33.0 percent in 1996 to 39.1 percent in 2006.

In all regions, women's share of employment in industry is lower than that of men. Among developed economies, just 12.4 percent of women work in industry, compared with 33.6 percent of men. Similar patterns exist for most regions; only in East Asia and Southeast Asia and the Pacific are the shares more balanced.

Service employment has increased for both men and women in all regions except the Middle East and North Africa, where the proportion of female service employment has remained the same over the 10-year period and declined marginally for men. For women, service employment has overtaken agricultural employment in half of the regions: developed economies, Central and Eastern Europe (non–EU) and the CIS, Latin America and the Caribbean, and the Middle East and North Africa. Agriculture remains the most important sector for women's employment

Table 5.7   Shares of Total Employment, by Sex, Region, and Sector, 1996 and 2006
(percent)

Sex/region	Employment in agriculture		Employment in industry		Employment in services	
Women	*1996*	*2006*	*1996*	*2006*	*1996*	*2006*
World	45.4	40.4	17.4	17.2	37.2	42.4
Developed economies and European Union	4.3	2.5	16.8	12.4	78.9	85.1
Central and Eastern Europe (non–EU) and Commonwealth of Independent States	25.5	21.6	22.1	19.7	52.4	58.7
East Asia	58.4	52.1	24.0	24.7	17.6	23.3
Southeast Asia and the Pacific	52.5	47.2	13.7	15.4	33.8	37.3
South Asia	72.6	64.5	12.0	17.7	15.4	17.9
Latin America and the Caribbean	14.0	9.9	14.5	14.3	71.5	75.8
Middle East and North Africa	33.0	39.1	17.7	11.7	49.2	49.2
Sub-Saharan Africa	69.4	64.2	5.8	5.5	24.7	30.3
Men						
World	41.6	37.5	23.9	24.0	34.5	38.4
Developed economies and European Union	5.8	3.7	37.3	33.6	56.9	62.7
Central and Eastern Europe (non–EU) and Commonwealth of Independent States	26.8	22.4	32.7	34.3	40.5	43.3
East Asia	50.4	45.3	26.2	26.8	23.3	27.9
Southeast Asia and the Pacific	49.9	46.8	18.3	19.5	31.8	33.6
South Asia	53.9	46.4	16.8	19.3	29.3	34.3
Latin America and the Caribbean	28.5	24.7	23.7	23.4	47.9	51.9
Middle East and North Africa	28.8	26.7	22.8	26.5	48.4	46.8
Sub-Saharan Africa	67.0	62.1	11.4	11.3	21.5	26.6

Source: ILO 2007, 15.

in East Asia, South Asia, and Sub-Saharan Africa. Proportions for 2008 indicate that "in Sub-Saharan Africa and South Asia, the agricultural sector makes up more than 60 percent of all female employment" (ILO 2009, 10).

One indicator of progress toward MDG 3 is an increasing share of women in wage employment in the nonagricultural sector. Although no target has been set, this change should accompany economic development as people move from being contributing family workers and own-account workers to being wage and salaried workers (ILO 2007, 10). Figure 5.9 examines the change in the share of women in nonagricultural wage employment (and the proportion of seats in parliament held by women) by region.

Figure 5.9 suggests that women's share of nonagricultural wage employment increased in all regions from 1990 to 2005. Europe and Central Asia saw a particularly significant increase (47 percent); the Middle East and North Africa had a 20 percent rise. The increase was greatest in highly urbanized, upper-middle-class countries (43 percent) and lowest in rural, low-income countries (30 percent). These data may not paint the whole picture, however: aggregate country data conceal inequalities within countries, and disadvantaged and excluded groups are less likely to be employed in paid nonagricultural work (figure 5.10).

Status of Employment

Women usually bear more responsibility for the family than men do. Although there has been some progress toward a more even distribution

Figure 5.9   Share of Nonagricultural Wage Employment and Parliamentary Seats Held by Women, by Region, 1990–2005

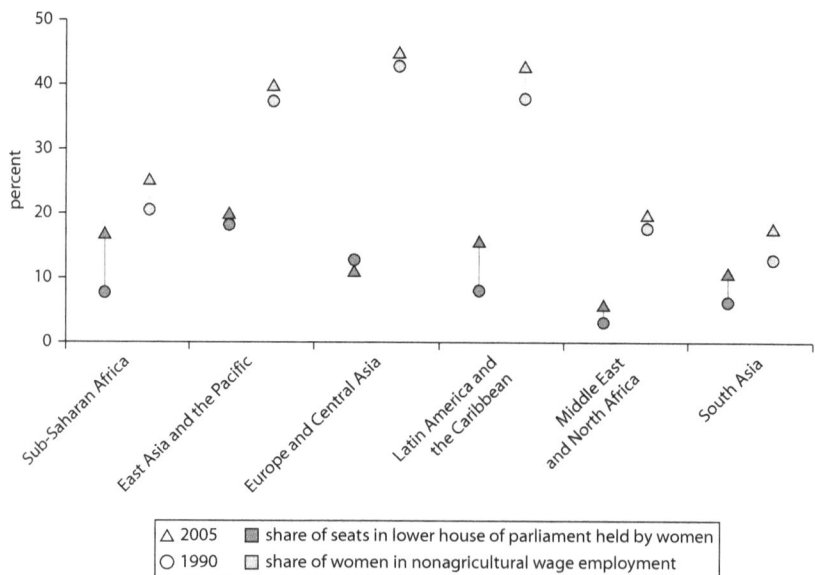

Source: World Bank 2007, 118.
Note: Regional averages were calculated using the earliest value between 1990 and 1995 and the latest value between 2000 and 2005 for each country. The averages are weighted by country population in 2005.

Figure 5.10   Share of Women in Nonagricultural Wage Work in Bolivia, Brazil, and Guatemala, by Ethnicity

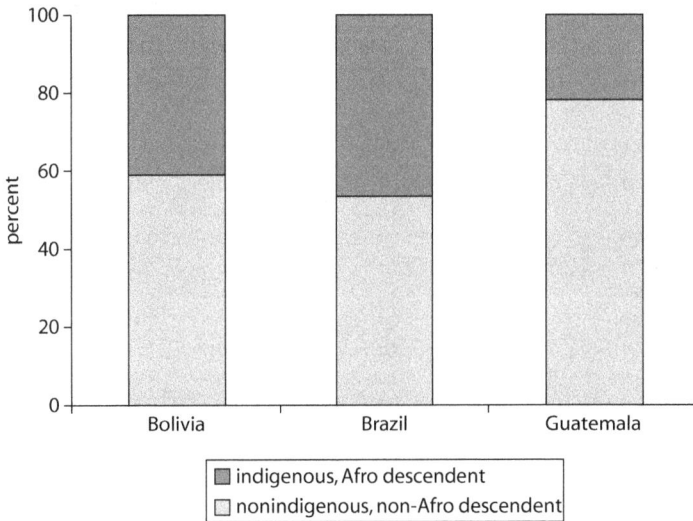

Source: World Bank 2007, 119, citing World Bank staff calculations using household survey data from Bolivia (2002), Brazil (2001), and Guatemala (2002).

of domestic work in developed countries, especially in families in which women are in wage or salaried employment, little has been done to relieve the domestic workload of women in developing countries, especially for women employed primarily as own-account or unpaid workers. As the ILO (2007, 10) notes, "the move from being an unpaid contributing family worker or a low-paid own-account worker into wage and salaried employment is a major step forward in terms of freedom and self-determination for many women, even though it does not always entail getting a decent job right away."[5]

Data disaggregated by gender on status of employment have only recently been made publicly available. The status of employment indicator places workers in one of three categories: wage and salary workers (employees), self-employed workers, and contributing family workers (family workers). In doing so, it provides a measure of the progress of female workers.

The trends suggest that, globally at least, women have made progress in the world of work. Table 5.8 shows the changes in employment status for men and women between 1996 and 2006. The share of female wage and salaried workers increased: 47.9 percent of working women were in wage and salaried employment in 2006, up from 42.9 percent 10 years earlier. The share of own-account workers also increased, from 22.4 percent in

Table 5.8   Employment Status, by Sex and Region, 1996 and 2006

Sex/region	Wage and salaried worker		Employers		Own-account workers		Contributing family workers	
Women	1996	2006	1996	2006	1996	2006	1996	2006
World	42.9	47.9	1.5	1.4	22.4	25.7	33.2	25.1
Developed economies and European Union	86.7	89.5	3.4	3.0	6.4	5.4	3.5	2.1
Central and Eastern Europe (non–EU) and Commonwealth of Independent States	78.5	79.0	0.5	0.8	10.2	12.4	10.8	7.8
East Asia	31.4	40.8	1.1	0.8	28.7	37.4	38.8	20.9
Southeast Asia and the Pacific	28.8	34.9	1.0	1.0	22.9	27.1	47.2	37.1
South Asia	10.3	15.3	0.5	0.4	16.3	21.7	72.8	62.6
Latin America and the Caribbean	66.6	67.5	2.0	1.7	24.2	25.6	7.2	5.1
Middle East and North Africa	47.5	56.2	2.4	4.1	17.1	11.3	33.0	28.4
Sub-Saharan Africa	13.8	17.0	1.1	1.4	49.0	42.3	36.2	39.3
Men								
World	45.7	49.2	3.8	3.3	34.7	35.9	15.8	11.6
Developed economies and European Union	81.9	83.1	6.9	6.9	10.2	9.3	1.0	0.7
Central and Eastern Europe (non–EU) and Commonwealth of Independent States	76.5	76.2	2.6	2.9	15.8	17.5	5.1	3.4
East Asia	42.1	48.7	2.9	1.5	34.7	37.0	20.4	12.8
Southeast Asia and the Pacific	37.6	41.4	3.1	2.6	41.2	41.4	18.1	14.6
South Asia	19.5	27.2	2.3	1.4	55.8	55.2	22.4	16.2
Latin America and the Caribbean	59.3	60.7	5.0	4.4	29.5	31.1	6.2	3.7
Middle East and North Africa	52.2	55.4	9.7	11.4	23.4	21.2	14.7	11.9
Sub-Saharan Africa	26.8	29.5	2.7	2.7	43.6	44.4	27.0	23.3

Source: ILO 2007, 16.

1996 to 25.7 percent in 2006; the share of contributing family workers declined, from 33.2 percent to 25.1 percent, during the same period.

At the regional level, progress is less apparent. In Sub-Saharan Africa, the proportion of women employed as contributing family workers increased from 36.2 percent to 39.3 percent. Although some progress was made in reducing the number of women in this category in South Asia, 62.6 percent of women workers were contributing family workers in 2006. More than one-third of women workers continue to be employed as contributing family workers in Southeast Asia and the Pacific.

Conclusion

In this chapter, we examined gender inequalities in the labor market. We first considered a number of reasons for the existence of such inequalities, including labor specialization and segmentation, and women's reproductive roles. We then examined the progress women are making in the world of work, as shown by LFPRs, unemployment rates, wage rates, and skills. We concluded by examining two measures of labor market performance: employment by sector and status of employment.

In summary, the chapter shows that women are making progress in the field of work, although gender asymmetries persist. Women are still underrepresented in paid employment in the world's poorer regions; girls are underrepresented in secondary school enrollment in the poorer regions; and women's productive potential is underused in all regions, with women more likely than men to be unemployed. Gender asymmetries continue to characterize wage inequality, with possible spin-off effects for future generations if parents decide that it is economically wasteful to invest in their daughters'—as opposed to their sons'—education. At the sectoral level, women are still more likely to be involved in agricultural employment, although more women have moved into paid employment, which is a sign of progress.

Notes

1. Collier (1994, 277) cautions against generalizing, given that "gender relations are inherently specific to social context."

2. The term *discouraged workers* refers to individuals who would like to work but who refrain from seeking work because they believe that no work is available, they have restricted labor mobility, or they face discrimination or structural, social, or cultural barriers.

3. For example, in Burundi, Rwanda, and Uganda, almost 60 percent of agricultural workers are female. In Ghana, where women workers dominate nonagricultural employment, most tend to be self-employed.

4. The World Bank (2007) references Anderson, King, and Wang (2003) for evidence on Malaysia.

5. The importance of this step is recognized in the UN Millennium Development Goal 3 (MDG 3), which aims to "promote gender equality and empower women." One principal indicator of movement toward this goal is progress by women in wage employment in the nonagricultural sector.

Bibliography

Agarwal, B. 1994. "Gender and Command over Property: A Critical Gap in South Asia." *World Development* 22 (10): 1455–78.

Anderson, K., E. M. King, and Y. Wang. 2003. "Market Returns, Transfers and Demand for Schooling in Malaysia, 1976–1989." *Journal of Development Studies* 39 (3): 1–28.

Anker, R. 1998. *Gender and Jobs: Sex Segregation of Occupations in the World.* Geneva: International Labour Office.

Barwell, I. 1996. "Transport and the Village: Findings from African Village-Level Travel and Transport Surveys and Related Studies." Discussion Paper 344, World Bank, Africa Region Series, Washington, DC.

Collier, P. 1994. "Gender Aspects of Labor Allocation During Structural Adjustment: Theoretical Framework and the Africa Experience." In *Labor Markets in an Era of Adjustment*, ed. S. Horton, R. Hanbur, and D. Mazumbur. Washington, DC: World Bank.

Collier, P., S. Radwan, and S. Wangwe. 1986. *Labor and Poverty in Rural Tanzania.* Oxford: Oxford University Press.

Corley, M., Y. Perardel, and K. Popova. 2005. "Wage Inequality by Gender and Occupation: A Cross-Country Analysis." Employment Strategy Paper 20/2005, International Labour Organization, Geneva.

Deere, C. D., and M. Leon 2003. "The Gender Asset Gap: Land in Latin America." *World Development* 31: 925–47.

Doss, C. 2005. "The Effects of Intrahousehold Property Ownership on Expenditure Patterns in Ghana." *Journal of African Economies* 15 (1): 149–80.

ILO (International Labour Organization). 2004. *Global Employment Trends for Women 2004.* Geneva: ILO.

———. 2005. *Key Indicators of the Labor Market.* Fourth ed. Geneva: ILO.

———. 2007. *Global Employment Trends for Women Brief.* March. Geneva: ILO

————. 2009. *Global Employment Trends for Women*. Geneva: ILO.

————. 2010. *Global Employment Trends*. Geneva: ILO.

Jacobs, S. 2002. "Land Reform: Still a Goal Worth Pursuing for Rural Women?" *Journal of International Development* 14 (6): 887–98.

Lastarria-Cornheil, S. 1997. "Impact of Privatization on Gender and Property Rights in Africa." *World Development* 25 (8): 1317–33.

Lewis, M. A., and M. E. Lockheed. 2007. "New Ways Are Needed to Educate 'Excluded' Girls in Developing Countries." *Finance and Development* 44 (2).

Morrison, A., and F. Lamana. 2006. "Gender Issues in the Kyrgyz Labor Market." Background Paper for Kyrgyz Poverty Assessment, World Bank, Washington, DC.

Oostendorp, R. H. 2004. "Globalization and the Gender Wage Gap." Policy Research Working Paper 3256, World Bank, Washington, DC.

Stotsky, J. 2006. "Gender and Its Relevance to Macroeconomic Policy: A Survey." IMF Working Paper WP/06/233, Fiscal Affairs Department, International Monetary Fund, Washington, DC.

Tibaijuka, A. 1994. "The Cost of Differential Gender Roles in African Agriculture: A Case Study of Smallholder Banana-Coffee Farms in the Kagera Region, Tanzania." *Journal of Agricultural Economics* 45 (1): 65–81.

Tzannatos, Z. 1992. "Potential Gains from the Elimination of Labor Market Differentials." In *Women's Employment and Pay in Latin America, Part 1: Overview and Methodology*. Regional Studies Program Report 10. Washington, DC: World Bank.

UNFPA (United Nations Population Fund). 2006. *A Passage to Hope. Women and International Migration*. New York: UNFPA State of World Population, United Nations.

World Bank. 2007. *Global Monitoring Report 2007*. Washington, DC: World Bank.

————. 2008.*World Development Indicators 2008*. Washington, DC: World Bank.

CHAPTER 6

Globalization, Gender Relations, and the Labor Market

Globalization refers to the increasingly free flow of ideas, people, goods, services, and capital across countries. It involves policies related to trade, finance, information flow, technology, job outsourcing, immigration, and remittances. It blurs the divide between local and international markets, and impacts employment and a host of other institutions, including the household. In this chapter we discuss how globalization affects gender relations at the level of the labor market.

Globalization and Gender Relations

Globalization affects the living standards of men and women through several transmission channels. Trade liberalization, for example, increases the flow of goods and capital across countries and contributes to economic growth. Between 1970 and the late 1990s, trade in goods and services as a proportion of world gross domestic product (GDP) increased by about 50 percent, thanks in large part to an increase in exported manufactured goods from developing countries in South and East Asia. The increase coincided with rapid GDP growth in these countries.

The impact of growth on the poor, however, depends on its sectoral composition. For example, agricultural growth reduces poverty during the early stages of development, as in China's decollectivization period and the Green Revolution in India. In both cases, growth benefited the poor and improved food security. In contrast, rapid growth that widens income inequality, which has occurred in both developed and developing countries during the past two decades, is likely to hurt the poor. Women are disproportionately affected by widening inequality, because they tend to earn lower wages and to have less education, fewer skills, and less mobility than men.

The Labor Market

The opening of an economy's borders has direct implications on the flow of labor both within and across economies. There are three main hypotheses as to why and when women find more employment opportunities under globalization. The *buffer* or *reserve army hypothesis* holds that more jobs for women are available during periods of labor shortages following economic expansions; these jobs are lost during recessions. According to the *segmented market hypothesis*, women find more employment when output in the sectors in which they are overrepresented rises more rapidly than output in the rest of the economic sectors. The *substitution hypothesis* posits that women's employment opportunities increase when they gradually replace men in jobs previously considered "male jobs."

Globalization may also affect the mix of formal and informal employment in the developing world.[1] Benería (2001) views formal and informal sectors as complementary. In African countries the informal sector contributes 40–50 percent of GDP. Women form most of the informal workforce in the developing world (Benería 2001), partly because their responsibilities in the home and persistent gender inequalities in education and the formal labor market confine them to the most flexible and lowest-paid industries.

Low labor costs, especially for women, may partially explain the outsourcing of services to developing countries such as China and India. Multinational corporations that relocate to developing countries provide employment opportunities for women, exploiting their willingness to work for low wages. To prevent multinational corporations from moving out of their country, some developing governments do not adequately enforce labor (including child labor) regulations, reinforcing lower wages for women.

Globalization also affects the flow of labor across economies. Historically, skilled labor migrated only across developed countries. Globalization, however, has resulted in a marked increase in skilled labor migration from developing countries to developed countries. Women's lower skill levels make them less mobile than men. That said, they are migrating in larger numbers than ever before. They tend to have lower-paying jobs, however—in fields such as domestic work and hospitality services—and earn less than men for the same work, even given the same education and skills.

Men tend to migrate abroad because of high unemployment rates locally, and they tend to remit larger amounts than women. These remittances go primarily to their wives for taking care of their children while they are away as well as to local income-generating activities. For their part, women migrate to acquire a greater level of power within the household, often remitting a greater proportion of their (lower) income than men. These remittances go not only to their immediate family but also to a wide range of relatives, with all of the money earmarked for family needs, including education and health.

The World Bank estimates that in 2004 migrants officially remitted almost $124 billion—twice as much as official development assistance. About 40 percent of Ghanaian and Nigerian migrants in the United States; 50 percent of all Latin American and Central Asian migrants; and 75 percent of Filipino and Indonesian migrants in Southeast Asia who remit money are women. Studies of the pattern and motivation of remittances indicate a positive impact for the household in terms of increased consumption, property investment, and better education and health care (Kireyev 2006).

The average cost of sending $200 has been reduced from an average of 15.0 percent prior to 2000 to 5.6 percent in 2006 (figure 6.1). Costs have fallen as a result of increased competition in the industry, which has stemmed in part from an increase in the number of money transfer organizations entering the market. The level of literacy among people sending remittances is very low; customers have very little information on the best money transfer organizations in their locality and the services they offer. Further cost reductions would stem from greater transparency in the industry, making it easier for customers to compare services.

Trade Liberalization

Trade liberalization has had a direct effect on gender relations, generally improving employment opportunities for women in developing economies.[2] The development of export-oriented manufacturing has increased employment opportunities for women in the labor-intensive textiles and clothing industries.[3] Of course, trade liberalization also leads

Figure 6.1   Average Cost of Remitting $200, pre-2000 to 2006

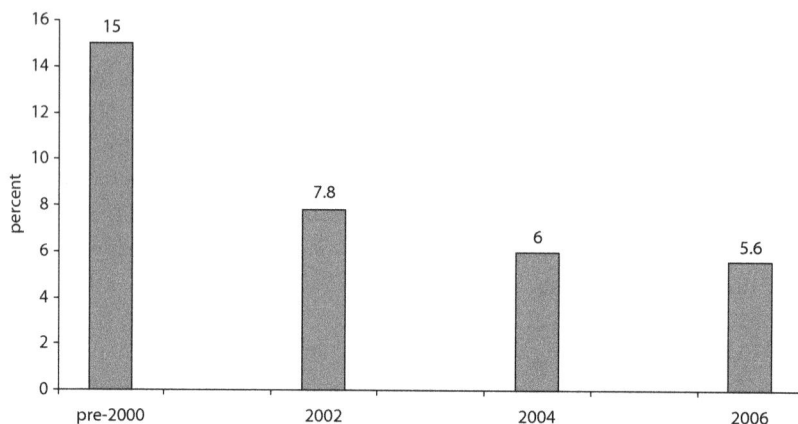

Source: MIF 2006.
Note: The average cost was $30 pre-2000, $15 in 2002, $12 in 2004, and $11 in 2006.

to a decline in import-substituting industries, which may offset some of the gains in employment in the export sector.

Trade-related gains in employment for women in developing countries have occurred in export-processing zones, in larger firms (that subcontract work), and in the informal sector. In Ecuador, for example, women benefited as flower exports increased. In Bangladesh about 2 million jobs were created in the textiles and apparel industry, most of them filled by women. Women still suffer from long hours, job insecurity, unhealthy working conditions, and low pay. Table 6.1 provides information on the share of women employed in export-processing firms in developing countries during 2003.

As shown in figure 6.2, the share of women employed in export manufacturing in selected East Asian economies is larger than in other manufacturing industries. The data confirm that trade openness contributes to the employment of women. But how do wages in export and nonexport manufacturing compare?

The Wage Gap
Trade liberalization has created employment opportunities for women; its effect on the gender wage gap is less clear. Some evidence points to a decline in the gender wage gap in countries in which trade liberalization has led to an increase in the share of women's employment, but the

Table 6.1 Women's Share of Total Employment in Selected Export-Processing Zones, 2003

Region/country	Total employment	Female employment (percentage share)	Main sectors of production	Zone exports as percentage of total exports
Africa				
Cape Verde	1,141	88		—
Kenya	27,148	60	Apparel/garments, pharmaceuticals, tea processing	80
Malawi	29,000	51	Textiles, cotton	—
Mauritius	83,609	66	Textiles/garments, food processing, footwear, jewelry, medical/optical/photographic equipment	77
Asia				
Bangladesh	2,121,000	62	Textiles/garments, food processing, leather, pharmaceuticals	60
China	3,0000,000	—	High-tech electronics, IT, pharmaceuticals	88
Korea, Rep.	39,000	70		—
Malaysia	322,000	54	High-tech electronics, food processing, IT, pharmaceuticals	83
Pakistan	410,540	82	Electronics, chemicals, toys, precision mechanics, yarn processing/garments, leather, food processing, plastic	—
Philippines	820,960	74	High-tech electronics, textiles, leather	87
Sri Lanka	461,033	78	Textiles/garments, rubber products	33
Latin America and the Caribbean				
Dominican Republic	181,130	53	Textiles, services	80
Guatemala	69,200	70	Services	—
Honduras	106,457	67		—
Jamaica	20,000	90	Garments, electronics	—
Mexico	1,906,064	60	Plastics, machine spare parts, packaging material, electronic components, wire, metal stamping, steel, chemicals, apparel, wood products	83
Nicaragua	40,000	90	Textiles	—

Source: Tran-Nguyen and Beviglia-Zampetti 2004, 23.

Note: — Not available.

Figure 6.2   Share of Women in Export and Nonexport Manufacturing in Selected Asian Economies

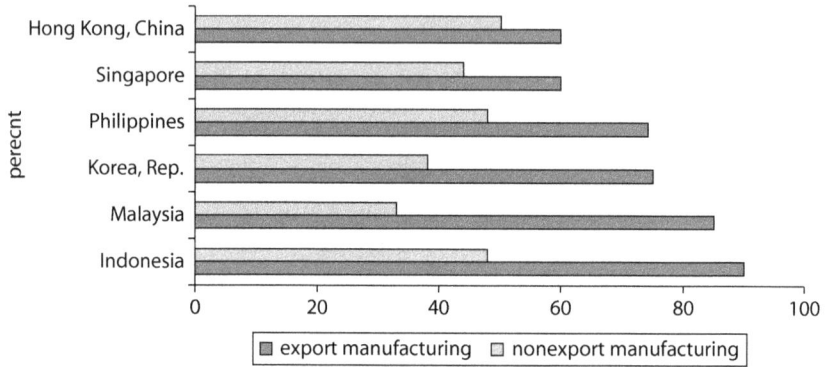

Source: Osterreich 2005.

evidence is "tenuous," according to Stotsky 2007. Oostendorp (2004) reaches a similar conclusion. Using cross-sectional data on the gender wage gap from 80 countries in 161 occupations over the period 1983–99, Oostendorp reports the following findings:

- The occupational gender wage gap appears to narrow as GDP per capita increases.
- Trade and foreign direct investment (FDI) net inflows narrow the occupational gender wage gap for low-skilled occupations (in poorer and richer countries) and for high-skilled occupations (in richer countries).
- FDI net inflows have widened the occupational gender wage gap for high-skilled work in the poorer countries.
- Wage-setting institutions strongly influence the occupational gender wage gap in richer countries.

The increasing extent of globalization also means that the interaction of exchange rates with trade liberalization can affect employment opportunities for women. A depreciation of the exchange rate in developing economies with a strong export base may benefit women by creating jobs, although the wage effects of the depreciation may dilute the gains. Exchange rate fluctuations also affect domestic investment and the prices of tradable goods and wages, particularly in highly competitive industries, such as textiles, garments, agricultural processing, cut flowers, and low value-added manufactured goods. Goldberg and Tracey (2001) find some evidence from the United States that exchange rate shifts affect the wages of women who remain in their jobs, the wages of women who change jobs, and the frequency of job changes. They estimate that a 10 percent depreciation of the dollar raises women's wages by roughly 1 percent. Women who change jobs see a greater benefit—an estimated wage increase of more than 2 percent—than women who stay in their jobs, for whom the estimated wage increase is only 0.75 percent. For both men and women, the effects of exchange rate volatility are observed most among less educated workers.

The Global Financial Crisis of 2007–09

The recent economic crisis placed a disproportionate burden on women, especially poor women, migrants, and minorities (Antonopoulos 2009). Although job losses affect both women and men, women are often laid off first, because men are traditionally considered to be the main bread-winners. Gender-specific implications of the global financial crisis include the following:

- *Greater unemployment.* Women are likely to lose their jobs first and are at risk of being hired last.
- *Lower wages.* Because they are likely to be dismissed first, women lack negotiating power in the event of wage cuts or reductions in hours of work.
- *Decreased remittances.* The drop in remittances from family members in developed economies affects women in developing economies, reducing their autonomy and control over family matters.
- *Decreased informal sector demand.* Economic crises tend to significantly reduce demand for outputs produced in the informal sector (including agricultural laborers, traditional artisans, weavers, and vendors). Women predominate in these activities and are therefore disproportionately affected.
- *Less access to finance.* Most clients of microfinance institutions are women: they constituted 85 percent of the poorest 93 million clients of microfinance institutions in 2006 (Daley-Harris 2007). Liquidity problems in the financial sector are expected to reduce women's access to such credit. This is particularly significant in Latin America and the Caribbean and Europe and Central Asia, where microfinance institutions obtain some of their lending from commercial rather than concessional (grant) sources.[4]

- *Increased stress and violence.* Soaring food and fuel prices add stress and hardship to families, increasing the incidence of violence against women.

The monetary and fiscal policies that countries use to respond to recessions can also disproportionately affect women. For example, decreases in tax revenues and official development assistance lead to cuts in public sector budgets. Reductions in spending on health and education reduce women's and girls' access to basic services. Girls may withdraw from schools to help with household work during times of economic crisis, reinforcing gender gaps in education. Higher unemployment and lower household incomes force women to turn to vulnerable and informal employment (including caregiving, which is provided mostly by women and girls). These coping strategies undermine long-term economic development.

Among the 193 million people unemployed in 2008, 112 million were men and 81 million were women. The International Labour Organization (ILO 2009a) estimated that the economic crisis would increase the number of unemployed women by up to 22 million over 2007–09. The unemployment rate for women was 6.1 percent in 2008 and was estimated to rise to at least 6.7 percent in the most optimistic scenario and to 7.3 percent in the most pessimistic scenario in 2009 (table 6.2). In most regions, particularly Latin America and the Caribbean, South Asia, and the Middle East and North Africa, where women often face higher barriers in the labor market, unemployment as a result of the economic crisis was expected to hit women harder than men. Only in East Asia, Central and Southeastern Europe (non–European Union), and the Commonwealth of Independent States (CIS) was the opposite true. In East Asia unemployment among men was estimated to reach 5.3 percent, 1.3 percentage points higher than the 4.0 percent rate predicted for women in the worst-case scenario for 2009.

Remittances constitute 17–40 percent of GDP in many countries, including El Salvador, Guyana, Haiti, Honduras, Jamaica, Jordan, Lebanon, Lesotho, Moldova, Nepal, Nicaragua, Tajikistan, and Tonga (Antonopoulos 2009). Women migrants are traditionally employed in "female" occupations such as domestic work and nursing and are more vulnerable to economic downturns. Accurate figures for job losses among immigrant workers are difficult to compile; anecdotes can provide a general idea, however. For example, in the metropolitan area of New York, where financial sector job losses reached about 80,000 in 2008, the ILO (2009b) suggests it is safe to assume that at least 40,000 domestic workers

Table 6.2 Preliminary Estimated Unemployment Rates, by Sex and Region, 2009
(percent)

Region	Women			Men		
	CI lower bound	Preliminary estimate	CI upper bound	CI lower bound	Preliminary estimate	CI upper bound
World	6.7	7.0	7.3	6.0	6.3	6.6
Developed economies	6.5	8.6	8.7	8.1	8.2	8.3
Central and Southeastern Europe (non–EU) and Commonwealth of Independent States	9.6	9.8	10.2	10.3	10.6	10.9
East Asia	3.4	3.7	4.0	4.6	5.0	5.3
Southeast Asia and the Pacific	5.6	5.9	6.1	5.2	5.5	5.7
South Asia	5.5	5.9	6.4	4.4	4.8	5.1
Latin America and the Caribbean	9.8	10.1	10.7	6.5	6.9	7.0
Middle East	14.0	15.0	16.0	7.3	7.7	8.1
North Africa	14.8	15.6	16.5	8.0	8.6	9.2
Sub-Saharan Africa	8.4	8.8	9.1	7.5	7.8	8.1

Source: ILO 2010, 46.

Note: CI = confidence interval. See ILO 2010, 79 for an explanation of the derivation of the preliminary point estimates and the upper and lower bound of the confidence interval around the 2009 point estimate.

lost their jobs (Antonopoulos 2009). Job losses are projected to be highest among domestic workers from the Philippines, the Caribbean, and Eastern Europe, who care for children and the elderly across the Middle East, the United States, and Western Europe.

Policy Responses to the Crisis

The economic crisis provides an opportunity to generate policy responses that address the disproportionate social and economic burden that women bear. When governments design and implement fiscal stimulus packages, they should consider explicit employment growth targets for women, recognizing the challenges they face in the labor market. In this context, an appropriate policy set should include the following features:

- *Gender-sensitive employment creation.* Fiscal stimulus packages should go beyond a focus on job creation in male-dominated sectors, such as urban construction. Instead, policy makers should focus on labor sectors that include more women. Investing in rural infrastructure creates employment and builds a foundation for sustainable growth. Furthering poverty alleviation through the construction and repair of farm-to-market roads, postharvest facilities, irrigation systems, potable water systems, and other farm projects provides long-term advantages to a large percentage of women in agriculture. It also provides opportunities for migrant women returning to the countryside and working as subsistence farmers.
- *Investment in social infrastructure.* Fiscal stimulus packages should include initiatives in education and health care that inject financial and human capital into fields with high female employment.
- *Increased credit lines to women.* Governments should subsidize credit and guarantee loans that foster job creation for women. Commercial banks that receive liquidity support from central banks should be required to maintain funding for microcredit, which is vital in the informal sector, in which large numbers of women work.

Conclusion

In this chapter we examined the impact of globalization on gender relations at the level of the labor market. As an economy opens its markets to the world, the initial impact on women appears to be negative, especially for unskilled women. Under trade liberalization, however, the evidence suggests a positive outcome for women. In particular, when an economy develops a strong export sector in manufacturing, increased employment opportunities arise for women, especially in the clothing and textile sectors. Although multinational corporations may generate new job opportunities, they also bring a higher risk of exploitation. Evidence that globalization improves the gender wage gap is tenuous, as is its effect on overall gender relations.

The chapter concluded with a discussion of the effects of the 2007–09 global economic crisis on gender, focusing on the labor market. Policy responses that could mitigate an increase in gender inequality are suggested.

Notes

1. The relationship between the formal and informal sectors can be caused by (a) the dualistic features in developing countries, where the formal and the informal sectors exist separately, with no direct links between the two; (b) structural factors, where the subservient informal sector is a source of cheap labor and goods for the wealthier and powerful elites; and (c) the high burden of regulations, which cause enterprises to resort to informality as a response to overregulation and control by bureaucratic governments that enact rules and regulations but do not enforce full compliance.

2. See Stotsky (2006) for a review of studies showing the positive impact of trade liberalization on women's employment.

3. Although export-oriented firms are concentrated in many industries, they are dominant in clothing and textiles.

4. Consultative Group to Assist the Poor (CGAP) Web site (http://www2.cgap .org/p/site/c/template.rc/1.11.12051/1.26.4005).

Bibliography

Antonopoulos, Rania. 2009. "The Current Economic and Financial Crisis: A Gender Perspective." Working Paper 562, Levy Economics Institute of Bard College, Annandale-on-Hudson, NY.

Aslanbeigui, Nahid, and Gale Summerfield. 2000. "The Asian Crisis, Gender and the International Financial Architecture." *Feminist Economics* 6 (3): 81–104.

Bajtelsmit, V., and A. Bernasek. 1996. "Why Do Women Invest Differently Than Men?" *Financial Counseling and Planning* 7: 1–10.

Bajtelsmit, V., and J. van Derhei. 1997. "Risk Aversion and Pension Investment Choices." In *Positioning Pensions for the Twenty-First Century*, ed. Michael

Gordon, O. S. Mitchell, and M. M. Twinney. Philadelphia: University of Pennsylvania Press.

Benería, Lourdes. 2001. "Accounting for Women's Work: The Progress of Two Decades." *World Development* 20 (11): 1547–60.

Daley-Harris, S. 2007. *State of the Microcredit Summit Campaign Report, 2007.* Microcredit Summit Campaign, Washington, DC.

Elson, Diane, and Nilufer Çağatay. 2000. "The Social Content of Macroeconomic Policies." *World Development* 28 (7): 1347–65.

Federal Reserve Bank of Dallas. 2006. *The Best of All Worlds: Globalizing the Knowledge Economy.* Dallas: Federal Reserve Bank.

Frankenberg, E., D. Thomas, and K. Beegle. 1999. "The Real Costs of Indonesia's Economic Crisis: Preliminary Findings from the Indonesia Family Life Surveys." Labor and Population Program Working Paper Series 99–04, RAND, Santa Monica, CA.

Goldberg, Linda, and J. Tracey. 2001. "Gender Differences in the Labor Market: Effects of the Dollar." *American Economic Review* 91 (2): 400–45.

Grabel, Ilene. 2000. "Identifying Risks, Preventing Crisis: Lessons from the Asian Crisis." *Journal of Economic Issues* 34 (2): 377–83.

Hinz, Richard P., David D. McCarthy, and John A. Turner. 1996. "Are Women Conservative Investors? Gender Differences in Participant Directed Pension Investments." Pension Research Council Working Paper 96-17, Wharton School Pension Research Council, University of Pennsylvania, Philadelphia.

ILO (International Labour Organization). 2009a. *Global Employment Trends for Women.* March. Geneva: ILO.

———. 2009b. *Impact of the Financial Crisis on Finance Sector Workers.* Issue Paper, Global Dialogue Forum on the Impact of the Financial Crisis on Finance Sector Workers, Geneva, February 24–25.

———. 2010. *Global Employment Trends.* Geneva: ILO.

Kireyev, Alexei. 2006. "The Macroeconomics of Remittances: The Case of Tajikistan." IMF Working Paper WP/06/2, International Monetary Fund, Washington, DC.

Korinek, J. 2005. "Trade and Gender: Issues and Interactions." OECD Trade Policy WP 24, Organisation for Economic Co-operation and Development, Paris.

Lee, Jong-Wha, and Changyong Rhee. 1999. "Social Impacts of the Asian Crisis: Policy Challenges and Lessons." Human Development Report Office, Occasional Paper 33, United Nations, New York.

Lim, J. 2000. "The Effects of the East Asian Crisis on the Employment of Men and Women: The Philippine Case." *World Development* 28 (7): 1285–306.

Loxley, John. 1999. "The Alternative Federal Budget in Canada: A New Approach to Fiscal Democracy." Paper prepared for workshop on "Pro-Poor Gender- and Environment-Sensitive Budgets," United Nations Development Programme (UNDP) and United Nations Development Fund for Women (UNIFEM), New York, June 28–30.

MIF (Multilateral Investment Fund). 2006. "Sending Money Home: a Scorecard for the Remittance Industry." Seminar on "Sending Money Home: Remittances and Transnational Families," Inter-American Development Bank, May 12.

Ofreno, R., J. Lim, and L. Gula. 1999. "Subcontracted Women Workers in the Context of the Global Economy: The Philippine Case." Paper commissioned by the Asia Foundation, Washington, DC.

Oostendorp, R. H. 2004. "Globalization and the Gender Wage Gap." Working Paper 3256, World Bank, Washington, DC.

Orozco, M. 2006. "Gender and Remittances: Preliminary Notes about Senders and Recipients in Latin America and the Caribbean." Notes presented to the panel on Gender Dimensions of International Migration at the United Nations, New York, March 2.

Osterreich, Shaianne T. 2005. "Gender and International Trade in Asia: Case Studies on Households and Workers." Workshop on "Economic Policy and Gender Capacity Building in East Asia," Surabaya, Indonesia, October 25–26.

Ramírez, C., D. Mar Garcia, and J. Miquez Morais. 2005. "Crossing Borders: Remittances, Gender and Development." United Nations International Research and Training Institute for the Advancement of Women Working Paper, United Nations, New York.

Sadoulet, E., A. de Janvry, and S. Lambert. 2002. "The Roles of Destination, Gender, and Household Composition in Explaining Remittances: An Analysis for the Dominican Sierra." *Journal of Development Economics* 68 (2): 309–28.

Santillán, D., and M. E. Ulfe. 2006. "Destinatarios y usos de remesas. ¿Una oportunidad para las mujeres salvadoreñas?" Serie Mujer y Desarollo 78, Economic Commission for Latin America and the Caribbean (CEPAL), Santiago, Chile.

Semyonov, M., and A. Gorodzeisky. 2005. "Labour Migration, Remittances and Household Income: A Comparison between Filipino and Filipina Overseas Workers." *International Migration Review* 39 (1): 45–68.

Spotton, Brenda. 1997. "Financial Instability Reconsidered: Orthodox Theories versus Historical Facts." *Journal of Economic Issues* 31 (1): 175–95.

Stotsky, J. 2006. "Gender and Its Relevance to Macroeconomic Policy: A Survey." IMF Working Paper WP/06/233, International Monetary Fund, Washington, DC.

———. 2007. "Budgeting with Women in Mind." *Finance and Development* 44 (2): 12–15.

Swamy, Gurushri. May 2004. "The Impact of International Trade on Gender Equality." PREM Note 86, World Bank, Washington, DC.

Tauli-Korpuz, V. 1998. "Asia Pacific Women Grapple with Financial Crisis and Globalisation." *Third World Resurgence* 94: 1–8.

Tran-Nguyen, A. N., and A. Beviglia-Zampetti. 2004. *Trade and Gender. Opportunities and Challenges for Developing Countries*. United Nations Conference on Trade and Development (UNCTAD), Geneva.

UN (United Nations). 1999. *World Survey on the Role of Women in Development*. United Nations, Division for the Advancement of Women, Department of Economic and Social Affairs, New York.

UNDP (United Nations Development Programme). 1999. *Human Development Report*. New York: Oxford University Press.

van Staveren, Irene. 2000. "Global Finance and Gender." Paper presented at the International Association for Feminist Economics (IAFFE) Conference, Istanbul, August 17.

World Bank. 1999. "Managing the Social Dimensions of Crises: Good Practices in Social Policy." Paper prepared for the Development Committee of the World Bank and the International Monetary Fund, Washington, DC.

———. 2000. *World Development Report 2000*. New York: Oxford University Press.

CHAPTER 7

Gender and Finance

Access to finance or credit is crucial for improving economic well-being; gender discrimination has hindered access for women in this area. The literature on this topic is slim and falls under the umbrella of the micro-foundation approach to macroeconomics.[1] It is concerned with the microlevel behavior of individuals that leads to macroeconomic effects of growth and development.

One of the main areas in which women have been given preferential treatment is microcredit. Women's behavioral patterns with regard to risk taking and repayment of debt have clear macroeconomic effects. As noted in chapter 2, women have a lower preference for risk taking than men. Although this may reduce economic growth, it imparts greater stability to investment and financial markets. Women's higher repayment rate reinforces financially stabilizing behavior for the macroeconomy.

The economic potential of women entrepreneurs is curtailed when barriers—social values, religious norms, cultural heritage, and institutional practices—hinder their access to finance. Although women entrepreneurs have a key role to play in strengthening and broadening the base of the macroeconomy and in bolstering international competition, they may face discrimination in obtaining financing to grow their enterprises. Women may be unable to meet the loan requirements of formal financial institutions because of these institutions' biases against serving women along with the disparity between men's and women's ownership of assets. Microcredit has many benefits, but a gap remains between the maximum loan microfinance institutions can provide and the minimum loan commercial banks are willing to make. This chapter examines the literature on gender differences in access to finance and credit and highlights the macroeconomic implications for growth and development.

Access to Credit

A number of studies point to the economic and social benefits of facilitating women's access to credit. Figure 7.1 examines the pathways by which increased gender equality in households, markets, and society translates into current and future economic growth.

Increased gender equality in households, markets, and society increases women's access to markets, education, and health and gives them greater control over decision making in the household. A number of studies identify the significant positive relationship that extra income in the hands of

Figure 7.1 Pathways from Women's Earnings to Children's Well-Being, Aggregate Poverty Reduction, and Economic Growth

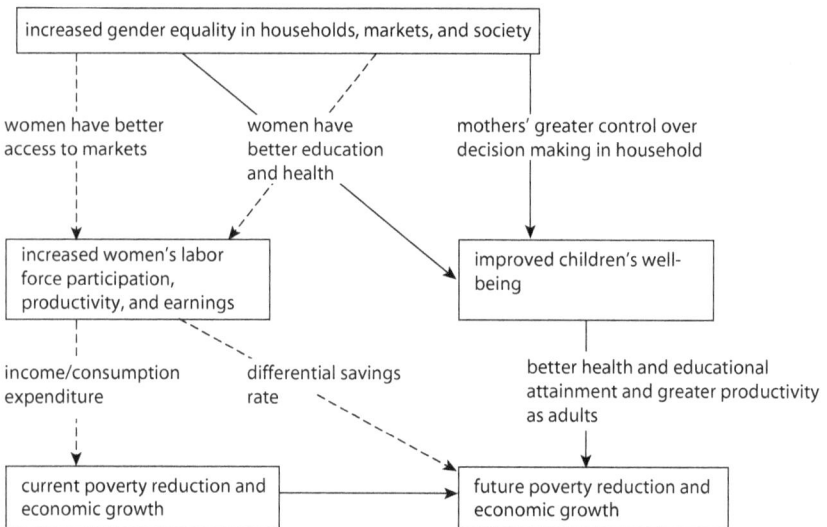

Source: Morrison 2007, 3.

women has on child welfare. Thomas (1990, 1997) shows that extra income for women in Brazil increased child survival by a factor of 20 compared with extra income for men and that the effects on child nutrition were four to eight times as great. Narain (2009) notes that a mother's access to credit directly affects the household, with positive implications for children's health and education.[2] At the macroeconomic level, improved child welfare translates into better human capital and by extension improved economic growth and development (as illustrated by figure 7.1).

Access to finance and credit empowers women. This empowerment is manifest in the form of increased earning capacity and control of household assets, resulting in greater autonomy and decision making within the household (Kabeer 1998; Khandker 1998; Pitt and Khandker 1998). The spin-offs from greater earning capacity, control over household assets, and voice in decision making are felt at the macroeconomic level. The provision of credit for women helps reduce poverty by enhancing the productivity of their enterprises and the profitability of other enterprises in which they invest (Kaur 2007). Some studies find that greater empowerment arising from borrowing enhances a woman's ability to sell assets without asking her husband's permission; such empowerment increased husbands' acceptance of their wives' participation in market-based economic activities (Agarwal 1997). Women's increased labor force participation, productivity, and earnings enhance consumption and income, which lead to economic growth and poverty reduction.

The literature also suggests that women's status within the household is enhanced when women have independent access to financial resources and are able to contribute to household income and welfare by increasing their level (if not their range) of economic activity. Using Malawi household data, Swaminathan and Findeis (2003) find that access to credit increases participation in farm and off-farm self-employment for women in male-headed households and in off-farm self-employment for female heads of households. Increased access to credit for women can therefore have a strong effect on national unemployment figures. Nanda (1998, 34), who assessed rural microfinance projects in Bangladesh, shows that "improving women's access and control over resources can potentially alleviate their health problems and enhance their decision-making within the household." Increased demand for health care can translate into improved national health outcomes, which can have a strong effect on growth.

Khandker (1998) examines the impact of borrowing from the Grameen Bank, the Bangladesh Rural Advancement Committee (BRAC), and the government RD-12 program on household outcomes such as per capita spending, net worth, boys' and girls' school enrollment, boys' and girls' height for age, contraceptive use among men and women, and recent fertility (table 7.1). The results can be summarized as follows:

- The impact of borrowing by women on per capita spending (household expenditure) is roughly twice as large as the impact of borrowing by men; increased per capita spending can therefore have a direct effect on gross domestic product (GDP).
- A 10 percent increase in borrowing by women is associated with an approximately 40 percent increase in per capita expenditure.[3]
- Borrowing from Grameen and RD-12 by women has a greater impact on child welfare—particularly nutrition and school enrollment—than borrowing by men, suggesting that women invest more in the human capital of their children than men do.

Table 7.1   Impact of 10 Percent Increase in Borrowing by Men and Women on Selected Household Outcomes in Bangladesh

Household outcome	BRAC		Grameen Bank		RD-12	
	Borrowing by men	Borrowing by women	Borrowing by men	Borrowing by women	Borrowing by men	Borrowing by women
Per capita spending	0.19	**0.39**	0.18	**0.43**	**0.23**	**0.40**
Net worth	**0.20**	**0.09**	**0.15**	**0.14**	**0.22**	0.02
Boys' school enrollment	−0.08	−0.03	**0.07**	**0.61**	0.29	**0.79**
Girls' school enrollment	0.24	0.12	0.30	**0.47**	0.07	0.23
Boys' height for age[a]	−2.98	**14.19**	−2.98	**14.19**	−2.98	**14.19**
Girls' height for age[a]	−4.92	**11.63**	−4.92	**11.63**	−4.92	**11.63**
Contraceptive use	0.40	**−0.74**	**4.25**	**−0.91**	0.84	**−1.16**
Recent fertility	0.54	**0.79**	**−0.74**	−0.35	**−0.74**	0.50

Source: World Bank 2001, 160, citing Khandker 1998.
Note: Figures in bold are based on coefficient estimates that are statistically significant at the 10 percent level or better.
a. Percentage changes reported for boys and girls height for age represent average impacts across all three microfinance programs.

- Borrowing by men has a greater impact on net worth, suggesting that men invest more in physical capital than women do. Widespread borrowing by men therefore has a strong effect on aggregate investment.
- Borrowing by men from Grameen and RD-12 increases contraceptive use and decreases fertility.
- Borrowing by women from BRAC and RD-12 decreases contraceptive use and increases fertility.[4]

Who Is Providing Finance?

In many parts of the developing world, access to finance and capital markets is considered a major obstacle to the inception or growth of women-owned micro- and small enterprises (MSEs). Table 7.2 provides a taxonomy of possible providers of financing for such enterprises.

Women use their own or their spouse's savings to finance their businesses. In Tanzania, for example, 66.0 percent of women used their own funds to start their business, 32.8 percent borrowed money from their spouse, 21.1 percent used credit from other family and friends, 8.6 percent received credit from a microfinance institution, 3.9 percent used bank credit, and 0.8 percent used credit from a moneylender. As businesses grew, additional capital needs were met by owners' savings (78 percent), microfinance credit (25 percent), and bank credit (10 percent) (ILO 2005c) (sums are greater than 100 because borrowers used more than one source

Table 7.2   Possible Providers of Financing of Micro- and Small Enterprises

Source	Nature of financing
Informal	Financing from family and friends, supplier credit, and commercial moneylenders
Semiformal	Rotating savings and credit associations (ROSCAs)
Nongovernmental organization	Donor funds provided to NGOs for distribution to qualifying MSEs
Microfinance institution	Delivery of financial services (such as microloans, microsavings accounts, microinsurance, and money transfers) to a large number of productive but resource-poor people in rural and urban areas in a cost-effective and sustainable way.
Commercial bank	Uncertain capacity to deal with MSE financing. Commercial banks are usually not willing to lend small amounts. A very low proportion of informal business sector operators have access to commercial banks.

Source: ILO 2005a, 26.

of financing). A 1999 survey of MSEs in Kenya finds that the main sources of start-up capital are personal savings and family funds (90.4 percent of initial capital and 80.0 percent of additional capital) (ILO 2005b, 22).

Narain (2009) notes that women in South Asia receive less than 10 percent of commercial credit. Women in Bangladesh, who contribute roughly 26 percent of total deposits, receive just 1.8 percent of credit. The International Finance Corporation (IFC 2007) notes that women in the Middle East and North Africa are more likely than men to fund their business start-ups and expansions from personal sources.

Semiformal financing is often carried out through rotating savings and credit associations (ROSCAs). A typical ROSCA comprises 5–10 members. At regular meetings all members contribute a fixed amount; every member then gets a turn as a recipient of the contributions. In some cases, outside cash is brought in through a loan from a microfinance institution and an interest rate is charged to borrowers. The ILO (2005a, 23) notes that ROSCAs "do not work as well when external capital is introduced, as this tends to make the lump sums too large in relation to the members' capacity to repay." In Kenya an estimated 76 percent of ROSCA clients are women.

Nongovernmental organizations (NGOs) play a key role in providing access to finance, both directly as lenders and indirectly as investors in microfinance institutions. The Women Economic Empowerment Consort (WEEC) in Kenya offers financial services (savings and loans) and training in business skills to women in the Kajiado District of the Rift Valley and two districts of Central Province (ILO 2005b). NGOs are also involved in microlending in Tanzania. Most members of the Tanzania Gatsby Trust (TGT) and the Zanzibar Fund for Self-Reliance are women. TGT's client base is 80 percent women; of the approximately 4,000 members of the Zanzibar Fund for Self-Reliance, 70 percent are women (ILO 2005c, 32).

Role of Microfinance

Microfinance plays a critical role in meeting the needs of low-income clients requiring small loans. Morrison, Raju, and Sinha (2007) outline three important features of microcredit institutions that make them particularly accessible to the poor:

- They typically replace the standard collateral requirement with innovative contracting arrangements that provide strong incentives for loan repayment.

- They greatly simplify and streamline loan applications, decisions, and disbursement processes.
- They frequently couple the provision of credit with microenterprise development and management training (see World Bank 2001).

The Microcredit Summit Campaign, an advocacy group based in the United States, estimates that the number of microfinance institutions increased from 78 agencies serving 9 million customers in 2000 to more than 420 agencies serving about 64 million customers in 2009. Many microfinance institutions are subsidized by governments, international donors, and private philanthropists, as well as by commercial banks, in the name of corporate social responsibility. Early microcredit agencies operated on a nonprofit basis and did not require collateral. They reduced risk by offering group guarantees, appraising household cash flow, and keeping initial loans small.

One of the main innovations associated with microfinance institutions has been the development of group-based lending: "Group-based lending replaces traditional collateral requirements—based on ownership of land or other physical assets—with a group-based lending contract, which uses social capital and peer pressure as a means to promote loan repayment" (World Bank 2001, 117). This development appears to have been particularly significant in facilitating borrowing by women. Between 1985 and 1994, the number of women borrowing from the Grameen Bank increased from 100,000 to 1.7 million (Khandker, Khalily, and Khan 1995).

At the policy level, politicians and the development community have embraced microfinance, with the predictable result that some of its merits have been oversold. In reality, most microfinance institutions are weak, heavily donor dependent, and unlikely to ever reach scale or attain independence. To achieve their full potential to serve poor households, they need to fully integrate with the mainstream financial system. Doing so requires financially sound, professional organizations capable of competing with commercial banks, accessing commercial loans, collecting deposits (which requires a license), and growing significantly.

Globally, women constitute a disproportionately large percentage of microfinance institutions' client bases. Women make up more than 80 percent of the client membership of the 34 largest microcredit institutions in the world (Morrison, Raju, and Sinha 2007). A number of studies cited in Morrison, Raju, and Sinha (2007) suggest four reasons why microlenders target women:

- Women appear to have higher repayment rates than men.
- Given that women are more credit constrained than men, they are likely to be more economically disadvantaged and unable to meet the requirements (collateral, minimum loan amount) of more formal suppliers of finance, such as commercial banks.
- Targeting women directly increases their social and economic empowerment, within both the household and the community.
- Targeting women aligns with the microlenders' social objective of increasing household welfare.[5]

In addition, some microfinance institutions focus specifically on women.[6] In addition to the WEEC Kenya has two other microfinance institutions that target women: the Kenya Women Finance Trust (KWFT) and the Women's Economic Development Corporation (WEDCO) (ILO 2005b, 26).

Microcredit has been widely credited with helping empower women by increasing their contribution to household income and assets. As pointed out elsewhere in this book, when women have greater control over assets in the household, they tend to save more and spend more on children. Therefore, access to credit can affect national savings and human capital. Some studies find that microcredit schemes increase empowerment, including status and mobility (see, for example, Hashemi, Schuler, and Riley 1996). But in some cases, women borrowers have only partial control over loans or relinquish all control to male members of the family (Pitt, Khandker, and Cartwright 2006). Other studies point to disappointing results for women's empowerment. Critics note the lack of substantial training and support services and the failure to provide women with greater ownership and control in microfinance programs.[7] Other criticisms include the inability of these microfinance programs to move women into profitable nontraditional forms of entrepreneurship and the marginal effect on income and household decision making. Empowerment refers to much more than increasing income (Kaur 2007, 11).[8] As part of a broader effort to raise gender awareness and mobilize women, microcredit institutions could provide an entry point to strengthening women's networks and mobility and increasing their knowledge, self-confidence, and status in the family.

Gender Discrimination

Understanding of the benefits of access to microfinance remains insufficient, and it is unclear whether gender discrimination limits women's access to finance. Indeed, the issue of access is difficult to separate from related issues, such as gender differences in usage of formal and informal financing, titling, access to collateral, the power of the household head, education level, and credit history.[9] Culture, religion, and the legal environment also affect a woman's ability to access finance.

The literature on gender relations and access to finance is not very substantial and is based primarily on case studies.[10] Using data on the loan denial rate and interest charged on loans, Morrison, Raju, and Sinha (2007) find no evidence of gender discrimination in the small business and housing loan markets or credit markets in developing countries.[11] In contrast, Essel's (1996) study of the Kakum Rural Bank in the central region of Ghana finds that men had more access to credit from this rural bank than did women. Essel reports that institutional and cultural factors played a role in this gender bias in credit allocation. Institutional factors include banks' rigid demands for collateral. Social and economic factors include (a) women's fear of taking risks (as perceived by women themselves); (b) women's lack of awareness of credit (perhaps because of their low education levels), leading to reduced demand for credit; and (c) skewed ownership of traditional resources (which can be used as collateral) in favor of men.

Institutional factors identified by women entrepreneurs in Tanzania included cumbersome loan procedures, high interest rates, and a 125 percent loan collateral requirement (ILO 2005c). Women also believe that loan officers do not take them or their projects seriously. In Kenya woman entrepreneurs face discrimination in the form of cultural factors that restrict them from owning fixed assets (ILO 2005b).

Among the social and economic factors that woman entrepreneurs identify as limiting their access to credit is their inability to accumulate the savings required to start a business. Women with low levels of education are unlikely to have accumulated savings from previous employment; women who do not have property rights are unlikely to meet collateral requirements.

Furthermore, although commercial banks are often not interested in loaning the small amounts requested by many women entrepreneurs, microfinance institutions often consider the same amounts too large. This gap represents a loss to the macroeconomy when enterprises that would prove profitable fail to attract finance for growth. In fact, one of the criticisms of microfinance is that some view it as part of a poverty reduction program rather than a business development tool (ILO 2005b, 25).

Conclusion

In this chapter we considered women's access to finance and credit. Gender studies suggest that men and women use finance differently. Women are more likely to spend on the household and on children. Although this pattern is positive, the reluctance of women to grow their businesses or assume risk beyond a certain point may have implications for economic growth. Most studies focus on whether gender discrimination prevents women from gaining access to finance. The results are mixed. Findings depend on other factors as well, such as the time period, economic development of the area, education, collateral, and skills.

The literature suggests that women have benefited from microfinance, which has made access to finance easier. Microfinance has been credited with empowering women within both the community and the household. It is not a panacea, and many other factors—social, cultural, economic— impact on women's access to finance.

Notes

1. The term *microfoundation* refers to the microeconomic analysis of the behavior of individual agents, such as households or firms, which underpins macroeconomic theory (Barro 1993, 594).

2. A study from Bangladesh shows that annual household consumption increased by 18 taka for every 100 taka borrowed by women (Pitt and Khandker 1998). Studies from Latin America show that men typically contribute 50–68 percent of their income to the collective household fund, whereas women "tend to keep nothing back for themselves" (Chant 1997, 39).

3. For all three programs, the effect of borrowing by women on household per capita expenditure is significant at the 1 percent level (World Bank 2001, 179).

4. This result contradicts other empirical literature that suggests that women reduce fertility when they are more empowered. Low-income women in Bangladesh may view additional children as assets capable of helping out with what are often home-based self-employment activities (World Bank 2001, 161).

5. "A growing number of studies show that when women are the direct beneficiaries of credit rather than men, the impact of credit on various measures of

household welfare is greater, suggesting that credit may not be perfectly fungible within the household" (Morrison, Raju, and Sinha 2007, 17).

6. In some cases, women may be used by male family members to secure a loan.

7. Kaur (2007, 11) cites Cheston and Kuhn (2002), Goetz and Gupta (1996), and Mayoux (2000) as critics of the view that microfinance empowers women.

8. "Empowerment is about *change, choice* and *power*" (Cheston and Kuhn 2002, 12).

9. Narain (2009) examines demand-side barriers and supply issues affecting women in their quest for finance, citing a wide range of studies that highlight the variables discussed.

10. Reliance on case studies makes it difficult to draw robust conclusions, as the studies are time and culture specific and reflect a particular country's stage of development.

11. Morrison, Raju, and Sinha (2007) cite Baydas, Meyer, and Aguilera-Alfred (1994) for studies on Ecuador; Buvinic and Berger (1990) for Peru; Storey (2004) for Trinidad and Tobago; and Blanchard, Zhao, and Yinger (2005) for the United States.

Bibliography

Agarwal, B. 1997. *Bargaining and Gender Relations: Within and Beyond the Household.* Food Consumption and Nutrition Division (FCND) Discussion Paper 27, International Food Policy Research Institute (IFPRI), Washington, DC.

Armendariz de Aghion, Beatriz, and Jonathan Morduch. 2003. "Microfinance: Where Do We Stand?" In *Financial Development and Economic Growth: Explaining the Links*, ed. Charles Goodhart. London: Macmillan/Palgrave.

Barro, R. 1993. *Macroeconomics*, 4th ed. New York: John Wiley and Sons.

Baydas, Mayada M., Richard L. Meyer, and Nelson Aguilera-Alfred. 1994. "Discrimination against Women in Formal Credit Markets: Reality or Rhetoric?" *World Development* 22 (7): 1073–82.

Blanchard, L., Bo Zhao, and J. Yinger. 2005. "Do Credit Market Barriers Exist for Minority and Women Entrepreneurs?" Research Working Paper 74, Syracuse University Maxwell School Center for Policy, Syracuse, NY.

Blanchflower, D. G., P. Levine, and D. J. Zimmerman. 2003. "Discrimination in the Small Business Credit Market." *Review of Economics and Statistics* 85 (4): 930–43.

Braunstein, Elissa, and James Heintz. 2006. "Gender Bias and Central Bank Policy: Employment and Inflation Reduction." Working Paper 06: 1, Political Economy Research Institute, University of Massachusetts, Amherst.

Buvinic, Mayra, and Marguerite Berger. 1990. "Sex Differences in Access to a Small Enterprise Development Fund in Peru." *World Development* 18 (5): 695–705.

Chant, S. 1997. "Women-Headed Households: Poorest of the Poor? Perspectives from Mexico, Costa Rica and the Philippines." *IDS Bulletin* 28 (3): 26–48.

Cheston, S., and L. Kuhn. 2002. *Empowering Women through Microfinance.* Research Paper 7/8/02, Women's Opportunity Fund and United Nations Development Fund for Women (UNIFEM), New York.

Coleman, S. 2002. "Access to Debt Capital for Women and Minority Owned Small Firms: Does Educational Attainment Have an Impact." *Journal of Developmental Entrepreneurship* 9: 127–43.

Diagne, Aliou, Manfred Zeller, and Manohar Sharma. 2000. *Empirical Measurements of Households' Access to Credit and Credit Constraints in Developing Countries: Methodological Issues and Evidence.* FCND Discussion Paper 90, International Food Policy Research Institute, Washington, DC.

Essel, T. T. 1996. "The Impact of Rural Banks, Lending Operations on Rural Development. A Case Study of Kakurn Rural Bank." M. Phil. thesis, University of Cape Coast, Cape Coast, Ghana.

Goetz, A., and R. Sen Gupta. 1996. "Who Takes the Credit? Gender, Power and Control over Loan Use in Rural Credit Programs in Bangladesh." *World Development* 24 (1): 45–63.

Hashemi, S., S. R. Schuler, and A. P. Riley. 1996. "Rural Credit Programs and Women's Empowerment in Bangladesh." *World Development* 24 (4): 635–53.

IFC (International Finance Corporation). 2007. *Gender Entrepreneurship Markets (GEM) IFC: Women Entrepreneurs and Access to Finance: Program Profiles from around the World.* Washington, DC: IFC.

ILO (International Labour Organisation). 2003. *Tanzanian Women Entrepreneurs: Going for Growth.* ILO Dar es Salaam Office and SME Section, Tanzania Ministry of Industry and Trade, in association with SEED (Small Enterprise Development), Geneva.

———. 2005a. *Support for Growth Oriented Women Entrepreneurs in Ethiopia.* Geneva.

———. 2005b. *Support for Growth Oriented Women Entrepreneurs in Kenya.* Geneva.

———. 2005c. *Support for Growth Oriented Women Entrepreneurs in Tanzania.* Geneva.

———. 2005d. *Support for Growth Oriented Women Entrepreneurs in Uganda.* Geneva.

IMF (International Monetary Fund). Various years. *International Financial Statistics.* Washington, DC: IMF.

Kabeer, N. 1998. "Money Can't Buy Me Love? Re-evaluating Gender, Credit and Empowerment in Rural Bangladesh." IDS Discussion Paper 363, Institute of Development Studies, University of Sussex, United Kingdom.

Kaur, A. 2007. *Women's Economic Empowerment: Meeting the Needs of Impoverished Women.* New York: United Nations Population Fund (UNFPA).

Khandker, S. R. 1998. *Fighting Poverty with Microcredit: Experience in Bangladesh.* World Bank: Washington, DC.

Khandker, S. R., B. Khalily, and Z. Khan. 1995. *Grameen Bank: Performance and Sustainability.* World Bank Discussion Paper 306, Washington, DC.

Kota, Ina. 2007. "Microfinance: Banking for the Poor." *Finance and Development* (June): 44–45.

Mayoux, L. 2000. "Microfinance and the Empowerment of Women: A Review of the Key Issues." Social Finance Unit Working Paper 23, International Labour Organization, Geneva.

Morrison, A. 2007. "Does Gender Equality Matter for Shared Growth?" One-day course on "Employment and Gender in the Shared-Growth Agenda," World Bank, Washington, DC, April 25.

Morrison, A., D. Raju, and N. Sinha. 2007. "Gender Equality, Poverty, and Economic Growth." Policy Research Working Paper WPS4349, World Bank, Washington, DC.

Nanda, P. 1998. "The Impact of Women's Participation in Credit Programs on the Demand for Quality Health Care in Rural Bangladesh." March 18. Johns Hopkins Bloomberg School of Public Health, Baltimore.

———. 1999. "Women's Participation in Rural Credit Programmes in Bangladesh and Their Demand for Formal Health Care: Is There a Positive Impact?" *Health Economics and Econometrics* 8 (5): 415–28.

Narain, S. 2009. *Gender and Access to Finance.* International Finance Corporation, Washington, DC.

Pitt, M. M., and S. R. Khandker. 1998. "The Impact of Group Based Credit Programs on Poor Households in Bangladesh: Does the Gender of Participants Matter?" *Journal of Political Economy* 106 (5): 958–96.

Pitt, M. M., S. R. Khandker, and J. Cartwright. 2006. "Empowering Women with Micro Finance: Evidence from Bangladesh." *Economic Development and Cultural Change* 54 (4): 791–831.

Storey, D. J. 2004. "Racial and Gender Discrimination in the Micro Firms Credit Market? Evidence from Trinidad and Tobago." *Small Business Economics* 23 (5): 401–22.

Swaminathan, Hema, and Jill Findeis. 2003. "Access to Credit and Women's Work Decisions: An Empirical Study in Rural Malawi." Working Paper WP 03–04,

Department of Agricultural Economics and Rural Sociology, Population Research Institute, Pennsylvania State University, University Park, PA.

Thomas, D. 1990. "Intrahousehold Resource Allocation. An Inferential Approach." *Journal of Human Resources* 25 (4): 635–64.

———. 1997. "Incomes, Expenditures, and Health Outcomes: Evidence on Intrahousehold Resource Allocation." In *Intrahousehold Resource Allocation in Developing Countries: Models, Methods and Policy*, ed. L. Haddad, J. Hoddinott, and H. Alderman. Baltimore, MD: Johns Hopkins University Press.

World Bank. 2001. *Engendering Development: Through Gender Equality in Rights, Resources and Voice*. New York: Oxford University Press.

———. Various years. *World Development Indicators*. Washington, DC: World Bank.

Zaman, H. 1999. "Assessing the Impact of Micro-Credit on Poverty and Vulnerability in Bangladesh." Policy Research Working Paper 2145, World Bank Development Research Group, Washington, DC.

CHAPTER 8

Gender Budgeting

Gender equality became a target of government budgeting only in the 1980s.[1] Governments' new emphasis on gender equality, commonly called *gender mainstreaming*, ensures that the goal of gender equality stays central to all activities, policy developments, research, advocacy, dialogue, legislation, resource allocation, planning, and program implementation and monitoring (Sarraf 2003). As the definition indicates, gender mainstreaming goes beyond allocating funds to gender-specific programs or projects under a government department dedicated to women's affairs. It refers to a set of policy guidelines and analytical tools that all government ministries can use to generate feasible gender-aware policies. As Stotsky (2006, 1) notes, "To be more useful, gender budgeting should be integrated into gender budget processes in a way that generates tangible improvements in policy outcomes."

The Fourth World Conference on Women, convened by the United Nations in 1995 in Beijing, helped initiate gender mainstreaming globally by calling for the integration of a gender perspective in budgetary policies and programs (Stotsky 2006). Since then, academia and various civil societies and nongovernmental organizations (NGOs), especially women's organizations, have sought to influence and generate support for gender mainstreaming in government budgeting. As a result, both national governments and multilateral organizations have begun to promote budgetary techniques and measures known as *gender-responsive government budgeting* (GRGB) or *gender-perspective budgeting* (Sarraf 2003, 3). This chapter examines the rationale for gender budgeting by focusing on GRGB and its expanding coverage since it began in Australia in the 1980s. It presents the analytical and technical tools and describes the approach used by a number of multilateral organizations promoting GRGB.

Why and How

Gender mainstreaming is a catalyst for comprehensive gender budgeting that goes beyond programs specifically designed to target women. Elson (2002a) remarks that government budgets are not gender neutral but gender blind, having different effects on women and men.[2] GRGB, according to Elson, "does not aim to produce a separate budget for women. Instead it aims to analyze any form of public expenditure, identifying implications and impacts for women and girls as compared to men and boys. The key question is: what impact does this fiscal measure have on gender equality? Does it reduce gender inequality; increase it; or leave it unchanged?" (2002a, 1).

Sarraf (2003, 8) describes GRGB as a "series of additional and analytical instruments [that help] one to understand and make a judgment on the impact of government budget programs in reducing the gender gap, thereby helping gender mainstreaming and ultimately gender equality." The need for GRGB is clear, given the discussions of gender inequality in previous chapters, namely, persistent gender inequality in the labor market; the macroeconomic implications of gender inequality, such as lower growth and weaker economic stability; the effects on household spending on health and education; and the indicators discussed in chapter 2. Stotsky (2006) also discusses externalities as a justification for gender budgeting.

Thurow (1971) shows that the motivation to address externalities can encompass equity as well as efficiency considerations. Public intervention may be justified if society moves to a fairer distribution of income or well-being. If gender equality results in a more just society, even without economic growth, public intervention may be justified. But choosing appropriate interventions can be difficult. Options include new taxes, law reforms, subsidies, and increased spending, all of which have implications for fiscal policy. "Governments can subsidize private activities that raise the status of women or reduce gender inequalities, or they can provide such services themselves, depending on the extent of the externality" (Stotsky 2006, 14). For example, governments can provide women's health care and education or subsidize private provision.

On the expenditure side, gender budgeting can follow one of three approaches (box 8.1). Gender-specific expenditures have been a part of most national budgets for decades. Such expenditures target specific projects and programs—public awareness campaigns, publicity campaigns on gender equality, and so on; they are usually housed within women's affairs ministries or equivalent organizations. The scope of these expenditures is thus limited and not representative of the gender mainstreaming approach. Likewise, expenditures that promote gender equality within public service are confined to government personnel policies. In contrast, general and mainstream expenditures are subject to cross-sectional gender analysis

Box 8.1

Types of Gender-Sensitive Government Expenditures

Sarraf identifies three types of gender-sensitive government expenditures:

- *Gender-specific expenditures* are allocations to programs that are specifically targeted to groups of women, men, boys, or girls, such as programs on prostate cancer or violence against women.
- *Expenditures that promote gender equality within the public service* are allocations for equal employment opportunities, such as programs that promote representation of women in management and decision making across all occupational groups, as well as equitable pay and conditions of service. This type of program is distinct from programs that promote employment of an equal number of men and women, as having equal numbers of men and women does not prevent a situation in which, for example, the 50 men in a company are managers and the 50 women are secretaries.
- *General and mainstream expenditures* are allocations that are not in the first two categories. Gender impact analysis of these expenditures focuses on the differential impact of the sectoral allocations on women and men, boys and girls. Although the analysis is challenging, because of the lack of gender-disaggregated data in many instances, these expenditures are the most critical, as more than 99 percent of government expenditure usually falls into this category.

Source: Sarraf 2003, 7.

and involve many government spending agencies. They therefore represent the GRGB approach.

Gender policy and gender impact analysis also affect the revenue side of the budget. Stotsky (2007) notes that in many developing countries, women are discriminated against for tax purposes.[3] She cites the practice of "assigning, for tax purposes, all non-wage income to the husband, regardless of who owns the property (embodying the assumption that a women's property belongs to her husband); or assigning larger allowances to men, reducing their effective tax rate; or applying a reduced tax rate on the same income" (Stotsky 2007,14).

Stotsky (2006) presents two hypothetical examples of gender analysis in a national budget that explicitly address the gender dimension of the policy, the means of execution, the resources needed, and the performance indicators (table 8.1). Her examples illustrate what GRGB could look like in practice.

Consider the sample objective of "expand primary education." The GRGB approach challenges the assumption that an expansion in primary education will be distributed equally across the population. A gender-responsive budget therefore responds to the inequalities in primary education for girls.

In practice, the GRGB approach demands many resources, including pre- and postbudgeting tools and the training of budget officers. Moreover, the gender surveys necessary for planning are limited in their scope and coverage. These concerns represent serious limitations for developing countries. Although many international organizations facilitate the process by providing technical and financial help, "[such programs] cannot cover the cost of training of a vast number of staff in the government budget preparation process, especially at the level of spending agencies of central government and several local governments as well as the cost of conducting meaningful surveys" (Sarraf 2003, 11).

Sarraf (2003) emphasizes the importance of pre- and postbudgeting tools for the introduction of GRGB (box 8.2). Prebudgeting tools include a gender cost-benefit analysis and emphasize a participatory approach to budget preparation, reflecting the influence of government expenditure on the female population. Postbudgeting tools focus on the impact of government programs for the female population and the contribution of such programs to improving gender equality; these tools also influence future prebudgeting tools.

Gender budgeting should form part of the macrofiscal framework of the economy, and its microeconomic dimensions should encompass spending

Table 8.1 Hypothetical Examples of Gender Analysis in a National Budget

Ministry	Objective	Gender dimensions	Means of execution	Budget	Performance indicators and benefits
Education	Expand primary education	Girls have lower enrollment rate than boys; goal is to equalize rate and achieve universal primary education.	Subsidize parents who send their daughters to primary school, with eligibility based on a means test.	Derived from estimate of number of parents who would use subsidy every year	Ratio of boys to girls in primary education and total enrollment rate of boys and girls Improved earning power for girls because of better education and other social benefits
Health	Reduce HIV/AIDS exposure	Girls have greater exposure to HIV/AIDS than boys, because of cultural practices that limit the ability of girls to protect themselves against unsafe sex.	Develop programs that teach men the dangers of unsafe sex.	Derived from estimate of cost of training health care workers to deliver this message	Changes in girls' infection rate Reduction in treatment costs and improvement in health and life expectancy

Source: Stotsky 2007, 14.

Box 8.2

Analytical and Technical Tools of Gender-Responsive Government Budgeting

The analytical and technical tools of gender-responsive government budgeting include the following:

• *Gender-aware medium-term economic policy framework.* This tool assumes and advocates for the presence and integration of a strong gender mainstreaming policy in developing the medium-term fiscal policy framework, through engaging local government authorities, traditional rulers, civil society organizations, NGOs, community-based organizations, and donor agencies on both the revenue and expenditure sides. The tool is based mainly on the evolving notion of participatory budgets, which involve beneficiaries and affected groups in the design and implementation of policy, programs and projects, decentralization of financial authority, the empowerment of local communities, and cooperation with key stakeholders.

• *Gender-aware policy appraisal.* This tool serves to appraise from a gender perspective, the policies and programs funded through the budget, which asks, "In what ways are the policies and their associated resource allocations likely to reduce or increase gender inequality?" The tool refers mainly to the annual budget preparation process by government officials engaged in the budget management system.

• *Gender-disaggregated beneficiary assessment.* This tool is a means by which the voice of the citizen can be heard. In these exercises, the actual or potential beneficiaries of public services are asked to assess how far public spending is meeting their needs, as they perceive them. A gender-disaggregated beneficiary assessment can be conducted through opinion polls, attitude surveys, group discussions, or interviews.

• *Public expenditure incidence analysis.* This tool estimates the distribution of government expenditures among men and women directly involved in government operations or immediate beneficiaries of government programs.

• *Gender-aware budget statement.* This tool is the government report that reviews the budget using some of the above tools and summarizes its implications for gender equality with different indicators, such as the share of expenditure targeted to gender equality, the gender balance in government jobs and training contracts, or the share of public service expenditure used mainly by women.

Source: Sarraf 2003, 9.

and revenues. The macrofiscal aspect of gender budgeting should address the effect of gender inequality on economic stability and its ramifications for the labor and financial markets. At the microeconomic level, GRGB encompasses spending and revenues. For example, greater spending on education and health programs could promote gender equality. In addition, Stotsky (2006, 16) suggests that "gender budgeting might have advice to offer on the means of financing a deficit, the use of public assets, or the division of responsibilities among different levels of government."

Country Examples

Since the mid-1980s, governments and civil society in more than 40 countries have tried gender budgeting, with international organizations playing a supporting role. These efforts have focused predominantly on expenditure, although some have focused on revenue.

Reforms differ across countries, reflecting circumstances. Stotsky (2006) references Budlender and Hewitt (2002) as providing the most comprehensive survey on gender-budgeting initiatives. Table 8.2 summarizes these initiatives in a number of countries.

In addition, the Women's Budget Group in the United Kingdom comments on the fiscal policies in each annual budget. In Mexico NGOs work with federal and state governments to support gender equality and poverty reduction with academic research.

According to Stotsky (2006), the initiatives have experienced mixed results. In some cases, they have failed to take hold, demonstrating the need for strong political support and the integration of initiatives into the general budget process. To summarize Stotsky (2006), gender budgeting should:

- Be incorporated into standard budget processes, so that it becomes fully institutionalized.
- Address specific goals, such as reducing inequalities in educational attainment, that have clear benefits and can be measured using even crude tools and data.
- Draw on civil society for support and assistance to subnational levels of government where relevant.
- Cover both spending and revenue.
- Avoid setting specific goals for spending on women-related objectives (unless budgets are severely constrained and such spending is well below what an unconstrained budget would otherwise choose), because doing so tends to reduce flexibility, making the budget process less effective.

Table 8.2 Selected Country Initiatives on Gender Budgeting

Country	Goal	Means of execution	Comment/outcome
Australia (1984) (federal and state)	Provide analysis of annual budget's achievements in relation to women and girls.	Focused on job market segmentation and need to reorient labor market programs to benefit women. Recognized role of women in unpaid economy as caregivers. Focused attention on nongender neutrality of dependent spouse rebate. Focused on disproportionate effect industrial restructuring had on women-dominated industries (textiles/clothing).	Budgeting for women (called the *women's budget statement*) was given formal status within the overall budget in 1987. It did not become institutionalized and diminished over time. Gender auditing remains in place in some states, but with no ties to the budget.
European Union (1994)	Adopt Amsterdam Treaty, which combines gender mainstreaming in all community policies and introduction of specific measures to improve women's status.	Created framework strategy on gender equality (2001–05). Goal is to coordinate activities and programs on sectoral basis to improve coherence by developing reliable indicators and a system for monitoring, evaluating, and publicizing results. Launched annual gender equality programs. Established structural funds.	Qualitative objectives established in five areas: the economy (linked to employment), participation, and representation; social rights; civil life; changes in roles; and stereotypes. Quantitative objectives are to increase female workforce participation to 60 percent by 2010 and to ensure that preschool education is available to 90 percent of children between the age of three and mandatory school age and to at least 33 percent of children under the age of three.

India (2000–01) (federal)	Target expenditure to women (four types: protective services, social services, self-employment, and regulatory, such as maternity schemes). Adopt pro-women expenditure (poverty alleviation and water supply). Use a benefit incidence analysis to construct unit costs for different public services (for example, education).	Target expenditure identified for women in the areas of protective services, social services, self-employment, poverty alleviation, water supply, and maternity schemes.
Nordic countries (Denmark, Finland, Iceland, Norway, and Sweden)	Launch pilot programs in each country to focus on gender analysis of government programs, develop a gender perspective on resource allocation, and integrate gender equality as objective in the national budget.	Budget contained assessment of gender distribution of financial resources in Finland, Norway, and Sweden; elder care in Denmark; and disability payments in Iceland. All countries attempted to improve collection of gender statistics.

(continued next page)

Table 8.2　Selected Country Initiatives on Gender Budgeting *(continued)*

Country	Goal	Means of execution	Comment/outcome
South Africa (1995) (parliament and NGOs)	Examine gender implications of departmental budgets.	Developed training materials accessible to a broad cross-section of population. Produced series of women's budget documents, including studies on various gender-related issues, such as taxation and spending programs, that provided useful elaboration of issues raised elsewhere, particularly on the revenue side.	Did not become institutionalized, partly because of lack of effective advocate in the government.
South Australia (1985)	Provide statement of women's disadvantage.	Evaluated activities with regard to their outcomes for women. Tracked implementation of government policy on appointment of women to higher-level positions within government.	
Spain (2003) (central and provincial levels)	Require that all government projects and rules include report on gender impact of measures taken.	Main document of annual budget indicated government's gender-related goals, such as integration of women in labor markets and social benefits.	Ministry of Labor Women's Institute developed guidelines for spending ministries to create these gender reports.

			The Basque Country Women's Office (Emakunde), in partnership with a private company, Infopolis, has put together a collection of materials on gender budgeting; the regional government has not launched any initiatives. A law in Catalunya mandating gender analysis produced few practical results.
Spain (2003) Andalusia	Mandate gender analysis in all laws of the province (per Law 18/2003).	Formed committee comprising equal number of men and women from the regional government. Made mandatory the collection of gender-disaggregated data and their presentation with the annual budget.	
Sweden (2003, 2004–09)	Require all ministries to develop performance measures and external evaluations every second year.	Appointment of strategically placed gender equality coordinators; organization for coordination in all ministries established; training provided for the Gender Equality Unit; program of continuous training and support for all officials involved in gender-related works established.	Results were presented to parliament in 2006.

Source: Authors' compilation, based on Stotsky 2006.

Conclusion

In this chapter, we examined the concept of gender budgeting. As called for in 1995 at the United Nations Fourth World Conference on Women, integrating a gender perspective with budgetary policies and programs is instrumental in achieving gender mainstreaming—a global strategy to promote gender equality. Since 1995 national governments and multilateral organizations have helped develop and promote budgetary techniques known as GRGB. The impetus for government budgeting was discussed against the backdrop of continuing inequalities in key social, economic, and political indicators, which provided the impetus for government intervention.

The literature, echoed by policy makers and analysts, decries the gender blindness of most policies. Gender budgeting requires assessing the impact of policy decisions on gender inequality. Does it reduce gender, increase, or leave inequality unchanged?

We also discussed approaches to gender budgeting, focusing on the expenditure side and examining pre- and postbudgeting gender tools. Prebudgeting tools emphasize the participatory approach to budgeting; postbudgeting tools focus on the impact of government programs on gender equality and on women in particular.

The chapter concluded with an examination of gender budgeting initiatives in a number of countries. Since 1984, some 40 countries have tried some form of gender budgeting, primarily on the expenditure side. The experience has been mixed, with most initiatives failing to become part of the institutional fabric.

Notes

1. Australia was the first country to introduce gender sensitive budgeting, in 1984 (Leadbetter 2003).

2. "What is clear is that there is no such thing as a gender-neutral government budget. For instance, cutting back on clean water spending may disproportionately harm women and girls because they typically bear the time and physical burden of providing clean water to households when it is not readily available. Similarly, increasing school fees may disproportionately reduce girls' opportunities to attend school, just as reducing a tax credit for child-care expenses may disproportionately burden women, who are responsible for the greater share of child-rearing activities" (Stotsky 2007, 14).

3. Slotsky also notes that many indirect taxes may be biased against men. Excise taxes on alcohol, tobacco, and gambling affect male-dominated activities.

Bibliography

Budlender, D., and G. Hewitt, eds. 2002. *Gender Budgets Make More Cents: Country Studies and Good Practice.* London: Commonwealth Secretariat.

Elson, D. 2002a. "Gender Responsive Budget Initiatives: Some Key Dimensions and Practical Examples." Paper presented at the conference on "Gender Budgets, Financial Markets, Financing for Development," Heinrich-Boell Foundation, Berlin, February 19–20.

———. 2002b. "Integrating Gender into Government Budgets within a Context of Economic Reform." In *Gender Budgets Make Cents: Understanding Gender Responsive Budgets*, ed. D. Budlender, D. Elson, G. Hewitt, and T. Mukhopadhyay. London: Commonwealth Secretariat.

Klasen, S. 1994. "'Missing Women Reconsidered." *World Development* 22 (7): 1061–71.

Leadbetter, H. 2003. *Gender Budgeting. What Is It?* Department for International Development, London. http://www.dfid.gov.uk/aboutdfid/organisation/pfma/pfma-gender-budget.pdf.

Ram, M. 2002. "The Gender Implications of Public Sector Downsizing: The Reform Program of Vietnam." *World Bank Research Observer* 17 (2): 167–89.

Sahn, D. E., and S. D. Younger 2003. "Estimating the Incidence of Indirect Taxes in Developing Countries." In *The Impact of Economic Policies on Poverty and Income Distribution: Evaluation Techniques and Tools*, ed. F. Bourguignon and L. A. Pereira da Silva. New York: Oxford University Press for the World Bank.

Sarraf, F. 2003. "Gender Responsive Government Budgeting." IMF Working Paper WP/03/83, International Monetary Fund, Washington, DC.

Sen, G. 2000. "Gender Mainstreaming in Finance Ministries." *World Development* 28 (7): 1379–90.

Stotsky, J. 2006. "Gender Budgeting." IMF Working Paper WP/06/232, International Monetary Fund, Washington, DC.

———. 2007. "Budgeting with Women in Mind." *Finance and Development* 44 (2): 12–15.

Thurow, L. C. 1971. "The Income Distribution as a Pure Public Good." *Quarterly Journal of Economics* 85 (2): 327–36.

United Nations. 1995. *Report of the Fourth World Conference on Women*, Beijing, September 4–15. United Nations: New York.

World Bank. 2001. *Engendering Development—through Gender Equality in Rights, Resources, and Voice.* New York: Oxford University Press.

Younger, S. D. 1999. "The Relative Progressivity of Social Services in Ecuador." *Public Finance Review* 27 (3): 310–52.

CHAPTER 9

Conclusion

This volume provides a framework for considering the intersection of gender relations and macroeconomic policy: *engendering macroeconomics*. The subject was first broached only recently; this volume presents the progress that has been made in a few years. The analysis is timely given the focus on Millennium Development Goal 3 (MDG 3), which deals with promoting gender equality and empowering women.

The aim of this chapter is twofold. First, it presents a summary of the preceding eight chapters, organized around four themes. Second, we note throughout the book that data and discussion were not sufficiently developed in a number of key areas. We therefore conclude this volume by suggesting opportunities for future research.

Four themes were considered in this volume. The first concerns the establishment of a background for engendering macroeconomics—the why and how of the subject. We argue that gender is a valid analytical category in economics and that macroeconomic policy would be enhanced by taking it into consideration. We showed that since the 1970s macroeconomic development has affected men and women differently in the developing world. Continuing with macroeconomic policies that are gender blind is inefficient, because doing so retards growth and development now and in the future.

In explaining why engendering macroeconomics is important, we discussed the data and tools available to examine gender relations. We noted that statistics and modeling are critical in making explicit the inequalities facing men and women. Only by having access to these data are policy makers fully equipped to inform policy, measure its effectiveness, and monitor the progress being made. Progress has been made since the 1970s in reevaluating women's work to account for unpaid work and voluntary work. Gender-related databases have been used to identify gender inequalities in terms of inputs and outcomes.

The second theme examines the evidence on how the differing behavior of men and women affects the key macroeconomic aggregates (consumption, savings, investment, and government expenditure). Household-based differences between developing and developed economies form the basis for analysis. Although a lack of appropriate data hampers research, several conclusions emerge, in particular for consumption. Women in developing economies show a stronger preference for spending on goods and services that contribute to the human capital of their children. Macroeconomic policies that improve women's control of household spending should therefore strengthen economic growth. This relationship between gender equality and economic growth is critical. We reviewed the growth literature as well as contributions from feminist literature. Several studies indicate that gender equality is correlated positively with economic growth (although it is, of course, possible that the causality runs from economic growth to gender equality rather than the other way around). This finding bodes ill for developing economies, where gender inequality is higher than it is elsewhere in the world.

The third theme considered was gender relations and the labor market, where gender inequalities continue to be most visible. Although significant gains have been made in women's labor force participation rates, employment rates, and skills acquisition, progress has not been made in all regions. We considered why gender inequality in the labor market is an efficiency issue with which macroeconomic policy should be concerned. In doing so, we highlighted the vulnerability of women workers and discussed progress toward MDG 3. We then considered the impact of globalization on gender relations at the level of the labor market, before examining gender relations and access to finance. We noted that gender discrimination in the financial market is less well researched than gender discrimination in the labor market. Although such discrimination is a microeconomic topic, it has implications for macroeconomic policy. Studies show that access to finance depends on a host of factors, including collateral, education, and skills. One initiative that has helped increase access to finance for the poor and for women in particular is microfinance. Some studies also credit it with empowering women within their communities and households. The fourth theme considered the connections between gender relations and budgeting. We noted the concern expressed in the literature and in policy circles regarding the gender-blind nature of most government policies. We also discussed the progress that has been made in this area and explored gender inequalities that continue to exist in key social, economic, and political indicators. Gender-responsive government budgeting is a relatively new construct and a critical component of gender mainstreaming, the global strategy for promoting gender equality.

Engendering macroeconomics remains a work in progress. Despite significant research on the interrelationship between women's empowerment and economic growth and development, there is a need for further analysis. Persistent gender inequalities—particularly in developing economies and with respect to labor market indicators—represent a brake on economic growth and development. Women's empowerment policies need to be mindful of household dynamics and their broader macroeconomic impact. Insufficient attention has been directed to these issues.

Much has been made of the improvements in child welfare stemming from women's empowerment within the household—justifiably so. But much remains to be learned about the role of other causal factors, such as parents' education level; the longevity of improvements; and their implications for growth and development.

We noted that in many poor households, men make the health care spending decisions for their wives. Yet we do not know if there is a causal relationship between overall national health outcomes and control over spending on health. The same question arises with respect to overall national savings versus gender control of savings decisions. Both areas require further research.

Most studies on gender-based differences in savings focus on developed countries. By contrast, very little information on gender-based differences in savings is available on developing economies. The lack of information has implications for women's access to finance and their ability to borrow. More information and better analysis of the information already available are needed.

Research has established that the high income elasticity of demand for education and health care among women and girls implies that economic prosperity would disproportionately benefit them by expanding their access to these services; recessions have a disproportionately negative effect. Additional research in this area is worth pursuing.

In many cases, assessing the short- and long-term effects of policies aimed at empowerment is stymied by insufficient or poor-quality data. Although substantial progress in data compilation has been made, many questions remain unanswered. The Gender-related Development Index (GDI) and the Gender Empowerment Measure (GEM) indicators compiled by the United Nations have been criticized on several grounds. For example, the GDI fails to reflect many development-related problems faced by women, such as access to nutrition, housing, and clothing. It also fails to differentiate between men's and women's disposable incomes. These criticisms provide areas for further research. Future investigation could focus on adjusting the GDI for individual disposable incomes and problems faced by women. The GEM has been criticized for using international data; national data would better reflect the reality on the ground. Collecting and analyzing such data represent areas for future research.

More broadly, domestic work and child-related activities are largely unaccounted for in national income statistics, making it hard to interpret cross-country gross domestic product statistics in terms of overall welfare. Future research focusing on ways to account for women's unpaid work would be helpful in addressing these shortcomings. One must bear in mind, however, that data compilation is expensive, in terms of both time and resources; gathering data for its own sake is not cost-effective.

The literature on gender relations and access to finance could be far better developed. Most cross-country databases do not track gender in banking services, hampering research in this important area. Future research could focus on more systematic exploration of gender discrimination in the credit market and development of cross-country databases that track gender in banking services.

To conclude, current data and resource constraints leave much room for fruitful research. Many of the empowerment studies are based on case studies. Although these studies have been beneficial in suggesting correlations, they are restricted by time and place. Recent work in development economics using randomized control trials may prove important for engendering macroeconomics. Although such trials are not without their critics, their methodology appears tailor-made to address many of the important gender-based questions that remain unanswered.

Index

Boxes, figures, notes, and tables are indicated by *b*, *f*, *n*, and *t*, respectively.

A

access to finance. *See* finance, gender
    and access to
Africa. *See* Middle East and North Africa;
    Sub-Saharan Africa; specific
    countries
AFROL, 35
Agenor, P. R., 59
aggregates, macroeconomic, gender
    and, 2, 49–63, 154
    consumption patterns, 51–58, 54–55*t*
    household composition and dynamics,
        49–51, 51–53*f*
    savings behavior, 58–60, 155
agriculture
    control of resources, gender inequalities
        in, 12–13, 81*n*1
    labor market, sectoral analysis of, 88,
        101, 102–103
AIDS/HIV and gender
    inequality, 12, 143*t*
Alderman, H., 50, 56
Algeria, gender inequalities in
    education in, 58
Amnesty International, 34

Asia. *See* East Asia and Pacific; Eastern
    Europe and Central Asia; South
    Asia; specific countries
Australia, gender budgeting in, 140,
    146*t*, 148*t*

B

Bangladesh
    education, gender inequalities in, 57
    financing
        benefits of improving
            women's access to, 127–129,
            128*t*, 134*n*2–3
        providers of, 130
    savings behavior in, 59
    trade liberalization and labor
        market in, 114
Bangladesh Rural Advancement
    Committee (BRAC), 128–129
Becker, Gary S., 6, 17*n*2, 50
Behrman, J., 50
Beijing World Conference on
    Women and Platform for
    Action, 33, 46*n*8, 139, 150
Benería, L., 6–7, 16, 17*n*–203, 72, 112

www.ingramcontent.com/pod-product-compliance
Lightning Source LLC
Chambersburg PA
CBHW050713280326
41926CB00088B/3010